To the Chu,
God Bless and may...
tribe in step

John Janosik

Mary L. Janosik

At the request of the author, all proceeds from the sale of this book will be donated to the Delaware Community Foundation, primarily for educational scholarships, through the Janosik Family Charitable Foundation.

Back to the Basics

THE
JOHNNY JANOSIK
STORY

by Johnny Janosik with Tony Windsor

To Order This Book

Back to the Basics - The Johnny Janosik Story
6634 Mill Creek Road
Laurel, Delaware 19956
1-877-886-1300 *(toll free)*
www.backtothebasics.us

Back to the Basics: The Johnny Janosik Story
Copyright © 2003
Johnny Janosik
All rights reserved.

Published by Fruit-Bearer Publishing
A Branch of Candy's Creations
P.O. Box 777, Georgetown, DE 19947
(302) 856-6649 • Fax (302) 856-7742
fruitbearer.publishing@verizon.net
Graphic design by Candy Abbott with Suzette Stewart
Cover Photo of Johnny and Mary Louise Janosik by Theis Photography
Printed in the USA by Atlantic & Hastings, Salisbury, MD 21804

All rights reserved. No part of this publication may be reproduced, stored in a retrieval system, or transmitted in any form or by any means—electronic, mechanical, photocopy, recording, or any other—except for brief quotations in printed reviews, without the prior permission of the publisher or author, except as provided by USA copyright law.

Publisher's Cataloging-in-Publication Data

Janosik, Johnny.
   Back to the basics : the Johnny Janosik story /
by Johnny Janosik with Tony Windsor.
      p. cm.
    ISBN 1-886068-09-7
    1. Janosik, Johnny. 2. Business enterprises. 3. Family-owned business enterprises—Delaware. 4. Life skills. 5. Philanthropists. I. Windsor, Tony. II. Title

HD30.29.J36 2003
658.403--dc21   lcn requested

Dedication

This book is dedicated
to the people of the community of
Laurel, Delaware.

When I think of the many family names that have been an integral part of the history and very fabric of this wonderful town, I am reminded of how very fortunate I am. As a teenager, I came to Laurel unsure of what my future held. This community embraced and adopted me as its own, allowing me to raise a family and develop our business in the "First State" and best state. Now, over 60 years later, I am proud that the name Janosik can be included on the roster of family names that make up this fine community called Laurel.

— *Testimonials* —

The true measure of success lies not in the fortune or fame we obtain in or own lives but, moreover, how we use the gifts and talents provided to us by God as a vehicle to help others. Johnny Janosik is an individual who has embraced this philosophy and has certainly used his talents to help those less fortunate. I consider Johnny Janosik to be a modern day hero. Born to poverty, Johnny has overcome great challenges throughout his life and today stands as an example of what individuals can achieve in this great country if they are willing to work hard and persevere. Johnny's dedication to education and his firm commitment to help assure that no child is lost regardless of his or her socio-economic circumstances is inspirational. Johnny Janosik stands as a sterling example of what it means to possess true success.

Dr. Benjamin Carson
Chief of Child's Neurosurgery
Johns Hopkins Hospital

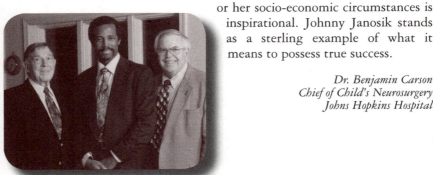

Johnny Janosik with Ben Carson and John Hollis

Johnny Janosik's history of helping others is a model example of all that charitable philanthropy is meant to be. The Janosik name is synonymous with compassion and generosity, and I am constantly inspired by the selfless acts of kindness exhibited by Johnny and his wife Mary Louise. The Johnny Janosik story stands as a testimony to hard work, dedication, and a willingness to face difficult life situations with extreme courage and wisdom. As extraordinarily successful as this man is in terms of his family business, it actually pales in comparison to the true meaning of success that he demonstrates daily through his support and encouragement of others.

John Hollis, Director
Southern Delaware Office of
Delaware Community Foundation

~ Special Thanks From Johnny ~

I could not begin to chronicle my life story without first sharing my utmost appreciation to the man who inspired me to write this book. John Hollis, Director of the Southern Delaware Office of the Delaware Community Foundation, first approached me about the idea of writing a book about my life in late spring 2002. The idea surprised me, and my immediate reaction was to disregard the notion completely. After all, who would want to read about my life? Besides, I'm basically a private person who doesn't want a lot of fanfare.

John, however, felt differently and was determined to pursue the concept of a book. Those who know John know that he is very convincing when making an argument about something he believes in. I suppose that's one of the qualities that led him to be so successful a number of years ago when he spearheaded a community campaign to build a Boys & Girls Club in Western Sussex County. In only a year's time, John's leadership brought the communities of western Sussex together in raising over $4 million to build the beautiful youth center that now serves our area's young people and families.

Undeterred by my lack of support for the book, John told me a story about a young boy who grew up in poverty and, by hard work and commitment to overcome many personal challenges, became a successful businessman. I was so impressed with John's story that it took a while for me to realize that he was talking about my own life.

In June 2002, I started resurrecting my past and putting my memories down on paper. This remarkable journey has allowed me to recall events and people that I had almost forgotten about. In short, it has been a wonderful, refreshing experience.

I think we all need a John Hollis to help inspire and encourage us as we dare to do things that may not otherwise have seemed possible. So, as this book unfolds, I say "thank you, John," for your belief that my story can make a difference.

I would also like to express my heartfelt appreciation to Candy Abbott and Fruit-Bearer Publishing for the professional and caring way in which this book was developed. Through this process, Candy has become a dear friend, and her work is nothing less than inspiring. She made sure all loose ends were tied and that even the smallest detail was addressed. It is with great sincerity that I extend my best wishes to Candy Abbott and Fruit-Bearer Publishing.

STATE OF DELAWARE
OFFICE OF THE GOVERNOR

RUTH ANN MINNER
GOVERNOR

December 2, 2002

Dear Friends:

As Governor, it gives me great pleasure to add my voice in helping dedicate "Janosik Park." I regret that I cannot be with you personally today.

As one of our state and region's most successful and responsible businessmen, Johnny Janosik has built a reputation for himself as an important part of the framework of Delaware's economy. For half a century, Johnny has distinguished himself by proving that good products and good service is still the way to satisfy his customers.

Beyond his business acumen, Johnny is a pillar of the community of the First State. From the charitable donations of furniture by Janosik's to Johnny's personal donations of time and money to those who need it the most, he has consistently given back to the community and invested in the future of our state.

This park will be a place of rest and recreation for generations of Delawareans. It is a fitting tribute to this wonderful man and there are few as deserving of such an honor.

Sincerely,

Ruth Ann Minner
Governor

Johnny Janosik has made many friends during his long career in Laurel. Two of those friends include Delaware Governor Ruth Ann Minner and Lt. Governor John Carney.

- Testimonials -

Delaware has been home to many successful individuals. Johnny Janosik represents the best of what Delaware has to offer. His never-ending stream of energy is an example and inspiration to us all as he makes it a daily commitment to work in the service of others. I am inspired by Johnny's desire to lighten the load of those people facing economic and social challenges. I have always been proud to serve the people of Delaware in the United States House and Senate, as well as in my two terms as Governor. My pride is heightened, however, as I recognize all that Johnny Janosik has done and continues to do to help make Delaware an even greater state.

The Hon. Thomas R. Carper
United States Senator

Johnny Janosik with
U.S. Senator Tom Carper

I would like to formally convey the great admiration and affection I have always had for Johnny Janosik. For about twenty years, Johnny and I were neighbors, and it has been my pleasure to be able to call Johnny a lifelong friend. Our friendship has even passed into another generation as we have daughters who are best friends and with whom Johnny and I are virtual second fathers. Quietly, Johnny has very frequently devoted his time and energy to helping his fellow citizens. Without any kind of public recognition or limelight, Johnny's enthusiasm and dedication in helping others has been extraordinary. I have always known Johnny to be there for me when I have needed him, as well as anyone else he knows who needs help. With his great knowledge of business practices, Johnny and his family have helped our community become a better place to live. Their assistance to those in need through the Good Samaritan Shop make it one of the best charity organizations in our state. While he may probably be best known for the very impressive business he has been able to build, Johnny will be better recognized by those that know him best as the great unsung hero of many in our area.

The friendship between Johnny Janosik and Delaware State Senator Robert "Bob" Venables has played an important role in both men's lives.

Delaware State Senator
Robert Venables, 21st District

ix

- Testimonials -

I have known Johnny over 40 years. During that time I have watched the Janosik family grow from the little TV repair shop and small furniture store on the Big Hill in downtown Laurel. This was only a small storefront. Johnny contacted Dukes Construction and had them refurbish the old chicken house where he is presently located. People wondered how he would ever fill up such a large building with furniture. The vision continued with more warehouses and other stores even north to Dover.

Never losing sight of his vision, the business grew to overwhelming size. But his desire to give back to the community that supported him continues. Johnny was instrumental in starting the Laurel Redevelopment Corporation, Good Samaritan, and many other worthy programs in Laurel. Very few people know how much the Janosiks have given back to their beloved community. It is very enlightening to see someone not only reach their pinnacle of success but share that success with their community. The members of the Janosik family have learned a great lesson from their husband and their dad and have inherited the same philosophy.

Dale Dukes
President, Sussex County Council

I moved to Laurel in 1973 but did not meet Johnny until 1993. That came about because my friend, Dr. Pierce Ellis, suggested that since I was retiring I should gather 15 people to discuss revitalizing Laurel's downtown area. When I read him the list of 15, he suggested adding one more, Johnny Janosik. Talk about adding a slugger to the team! He has proven to be Bonds, Ruth and Sosa all wrapped into one.

In the ten years of its existence, the Laurel Redevelopment Corporation (LRC) has met almost every Thursday. Johnny has missed very few of these meetings, and then only due to illness or family commitments. Many of the meetings were mundane until Johnny came bouncing up the steps with his never-ending agenda. His energy and enthusiasm appear to be endless.

He has done so many, many things for the LRC that to cite one does an injustice to the others. But one project stands out that is what I call "Janosik Park." This is the park in LaurelTown that Johnny almost single-handedly created, from the sprinkler system to the installation of the brick sidewalks. Johnny even cuts the grass. To top it off, he may have even solved a major problem we were having with an overpopulation of geese.

John's efforts on behalf of the LRC are more than enough to make him an extraordinary person—not to mention his other work for the Laurel Chamber of Commerce, the Hope House, the Good Samaritan, and countless other projects. There are many individuals who have benefited from the help of Johnny Janosik. In spite of all of his accomplishments, Johnny is a very humble man who is quick to show appreciation and recognition for others.

Where there is a good man, and Johnny certainly is a good man, there is almost certain to be a good woman. Mary Janosik is that good woman. I consider Johnny and Mary to be God's gift to the community of Laurel.

Bob Thompson
Laurel Redevelopment Corporation

- Testimonials -

The success of a man cannot be measured only by material possessions and monetary worth. Success is best measured by the accomplishments and magnitude of a person's many dreams and the sharing of heartfelt compassion for the well-being of others. This is the measure of success that makes Johnny Janosik an outstanding individual whom I greatly appreciate and admire.
Sheila Callaway, Management, Johnny Janosik, Inc.

Small in stature, humble in appearance, enormous in compassion. This is the most appropriate way I can describe Johnny Janosik. If you are searching for the true meaning of his success, you only need to ask the many people whose lives his generosity has touched. The faith that he has given me has allowed me to grow personally as well as professionally, and for that I could never repay him.
Dawn Haynes, Management, Johnny Janosik, Inc.

Dynamic, caring, a visionary who (with the dedication and drive of his wife Mary) have made this a top-notch company. His uncanny ability to handle multiple tasks while never losing sight of his goals is a trait worthy of emulation. His charitable contributions of money, furniture, bedding, and automobiles to needy individuals depicts a side of him that most people never see. That's because he doesn't do it for recognition; he does it because it's the right thing to do. Since becoming a member of this highly talented team, my abilities have grown to a higher level, and I'm motivated to strive even harder to accomplish my goals.
Norman Narcissa, Management, Johnny Janosik, Inc.

I was always taught that "not succeeding" is not failing—failing is not "doing your best" at whatever you choose to do. Johnny Janosik not only acknowledges and appreciates your best, he encourages it. His work ethic and giving back to the community have earned the respect of all who know him. You would have to look no further than Johnny Janosik for a role model.
Ginger Ayotte, Management, Johnny Janosik, Inc.

Johnny Janosik is a man of integrity and honesty. He has had the vision to guide his business in the most positive ways. He and his wife, Mary, have strong family values, and they have never undertaken a job that they did not accomplish. He cares for his employees and the people of the community. He contributes large amounts of time and money to people less fortunate and in need. I am proud to have worked for them since January 1967.
Beverly Hastings, Management, Johnny Janosik, Inc.

You have been and continue to be a mentor to many. Your enthusiasm, wisdom and vision have been admired by all. You are so successful, yet so humble. You may be a small man in stature, but your heart is bigger than all of ours put together. Thanks for being you and sharing your many gifts with others.
Debi Quillen, Management, Johnny Janosik, Inc.

- Testimonials -

I am honored that Johnny Janosik has referred to me as an influence in his life. I recall those days in the early 1960s when I would stop at Johnny's store on Market Street and chat on my way to the office. It was evident even during those early days that he was destined to do great things. I am proud to call Johnny Janosik a friend and appreciate all that he has done for our community. His generosity and compassion for other people are traits to be admired and provide a wonderful model to which all should aspire. As a two-term governor for the State of Delaware, I have always been proud to have had the opportunity to serve the people of this great State. Delaware has been home to some extraordinary individuals whose selfless acts of compassion have provided hope and reassurance to those in need. Johnny Janosik is one of those extraordinary individuals, and Laurel is indeed fortunate to have him.

The Honorable Elbert Carvel
Former Governor of the State of Delaware

When I think of Johnny Janosik, I have to go back some 38 years to the early days of my marriage. Just getting started as we called it back then, we lived in a $45-a-month rental and wanted all the things a young family could want. An air-conditioner seemed to be a necessity for the second summer of our marriage, so up to Johnny Janosik's Furniture Store Kay and I went. Johnny went over the details with us and almost immediately we had this huge 10,000 BTU (or whatever they were called) air-conditioner in our window.

"This will cost you less than two small ones," Johnny said. "However, if it doesn't cool the house good enough, let me know by Monday morning, and I'll put in the two smaller ones at each end of the house."

It worked fine, and over the years we bought many things from him; but it was that day and Johnny's individual attention that won us over. In the last few years, I have been around Johnny much more through community endeavors and functions, and one thing that is always the same about Johnny is he will never ask you to do something that he would not do himself.

One funny story from a couple of years ago involved Johnny's work ethic. As I looked out the window of my antique store, there was Johnny on this sweltering, hot August day working the flower beds at R.J. Riverside, one of the Laurel Redevelopment Corporation's projects. I walked out of my air-conditioned building and boldly said, "Johnny why are you doing this? You could be out on the golf course having a good time."

"Golf course? *This* is my golf course. I enjoy this," Johnny said as he continued to work. As I walked back to the store I realized something very valuable: enjoyment in life is not in the leisure of a person's life but in the enjoyment of what we do. Johnny Janosik has always enjoyed the hands-on approach to work. It's no wonder that he has no inhibitions in asking anyone to do anything.

Johnny has made a big difference in Laurel. His business has provided more than 300 jobs, and his resourcefulness and dedication to his town of Laurel have always been great assets!

Pat Murphy, Vice-President
Morning Star Publications, Inc.

- Testimonials -

It is a privilege to have been asked to write this acknowledgement of John Janosik. I have the honor and pleasure of working with this man on most Tuesday and Thursday mornings as part of the maintenance Cardiovascular/Pulmonary Rehabilitation Program at Peninsula Regional Medical Center, Salisbury, Maryland. It does not come as a surprise that John confronts and takes personal accountability for his own health in much the same manner and determination that he had in building Johnny Janosik Furniture, Laurel Redevelopment Corporation, the Good Samaritan, the Hope House, and the Janosik Family Charitable Foundation.

I first met John following his open-heart surgery, while completing the preliminary assessments for entry into the Phase II Cardiac Rehabilitation Program. What impressed me most was his "let's get the program going" approach. I was most interested in knowing his progress and what he could do to lessen the likelihood of having to undergo the surgery again.

John was then tracked into the maintenance program where the class time was more to his liking and schedule—6:45 a.m. Yes, John likes to get things done early, and he is the first to say that one cannot accomplish a good day's work by lying in bed. He told me once that a sign of a successful person is someone who likes to get the day started early and who is then driven to accomplish all that he or she can during that precious day.

When asked if I thought the book would be of value to others, I responded with an unquestionable YES! I think the following "lessons learned" are a value goal for all of us to strive toward in living our lives happily and successfully:

- Have a vision
- Learn from experiences
- Ask for help
- Be kind
- Keep busy
- Appreciate what you have and the people around you
- Pray, and finally
- Go Back to the Basics

By reading this book, I learned a little more about this man who is genuinely kind to everyone he meets. Thank you, John, for being a part of the program; but, more importantly, thank you for the kindness you have shown to me.

Jeanne E. Ruff, MS, RCEP, FAACVPR
Director, Cardiovascular/Pulmonary Rehabilitation and Health Promotion,
Peninsula Regional Medical Center, Salisbury, MD

Proverb 29:18 tells us *where there is no vision, people perish*. Sadly, in much of life today, people lack vision and, therefore, have little or no concern for the welfare of others. Having had the opportunity over the years to know and to work with Johnny, I have found him to exemplify the true description of a person with great vision. His concern, his dedication, his commitment, his reaction to his fellowman and to his community are examples of how much he cares. Johnny sees the need, and he sets forth the effort to fill that need. Our community and the people in it are a great concern to this man—a man of great compassion and vision, Johnny Janosik.

Dale Boyce, Honorary Board Member
of the Laurel Good Samaritan Organization

- Testimonials -

It all began in my early teens. My Uncle Ralph Gootee helped Johnny repair TVs when he first started in business. I met Johnny a few times, and he seemed okay to me. Later on, still in my teens, I helped my Uncle Bobby Gootee put up TV antennas on the side for Johnny. Johnny put up a lot of them up around the area. It seems the storms were always blowing them down. I don't know how many, but I'll bet Johnny does.

Through the years, I dealt with Johnny as his business grew. I bought CB radios, refrigerators, washers, TV, furniture, carpet, wood stoves, and on I could go. We would talk about whatever it was I wanted. He would be excited about it, and so would I. Johnny always had vision! There was something about him—I just plain liked Johnny. He always treated me more than fair.

In the early seventies I started working on the side doing painting and repairs while working full-time for Dukes Construction. I did a few little things for John. In 1975, with the blessing of and encouragement from my boss, Ross Dukes, I started my own full-time business. Through the years I did a lot of work for John. I've worked for him personally on his home, his business, and other projects. He has been such a positive force in my life these past 40-plus years.

Johnny was always an encourager to me. "You can do it, Donald!" Forceful, but at the same time, patient. "Okay, Don, do the best you can." To the point, "Now, Don, here is how I want it done." You did it the way he wanted, and there was never a problem. He has a knack for sharing his vision for the things he wants to do and getting you excited along with him. Like when he first got into furniture on Market Street. When he took me to the chicken house I thought, *he has surely lost his mind this time.* I thought the same thing when he took me to the little old house on the hill in Portsville, which is now such a beautiful home place for Johnny and Mary. Thanks, John, for helping me make it in the world of business.

I've worked with John on many community projects, too. Because I know Johnny, people will say, "Don, will you ask John for this or that?" I have never asked Johnny for anything that he has ever said no! John has never forgotten were he came from. He is a compassionate man for those less fortunate. John is a man that will listen to you. He is a man that will come to you in private and ask for advice. I know personally what John has done for the community of Laurel and for me that most people don't. He is one of the most giving men I know. Whether it is his time, talent, encouragement, compassion or money, he always has been and still is that man today.

To Johnny and his lovely wife Mary Louise, thank you for all you have done to make this a better place to live because of your commitment to God, country, and your fellow man. Most of all, I thank you for being such a positive influence through the years in my life. I love you both and God bless!

Donald Dykes, President
Laurel Good Samaritan Aid Organization

Table of Contents

Foreword xvii

Chapter 1 - Starting at the Bottom 1

Chapter 2 - Leaving Poverty, Heading for Uncertainty. 7

Chapter 3 - The Sounds of Guns and War. 15

Chapter 4 - Plotting a Course – Choosing a Partner. 25

Chapter 5 - Meeting Challenges, Facing Adversities. 33

Chapter 6 - Don't Forget Who Brung You to the Dance 45

Chapter 7 - Remaining 'Under the Influence' 55

Chapter 8 - They Keep Me on Track 69

Chapter 9 - Truth is the Best Defense 79

Chapter 10 - More Lives Than a Cat 91

Chapter 11 - Looking Back to Find the Future. 101

Chapter 12 - A Hand Up, Not a Hand Out. 111

Chapter 13 - You Can Never Go Home 123

Chapter 14 - Concluding Thoughts 135

Testimonials

Few people can lay claim to possessing the extraordinary measure of humanity that has been demonstrated over the years by Johnny Janosik. Almost daily he sets out to find someone who needs a helping hand and works to bring about resolve in their situation. As a member of the Laurel Redevelopment Corporation, Johnny does not recognize the words "can't do." His energy is boundless, and he stays with a project from concept to completion. There are not enough words in my vocabulary to express the deep sense of appreciation I have for the honor of calling Johnny Janosik my friend. He is a daily inspiration to me and so many others, and the Laurel community is truly fortunate to have him.

*Bob Durham, President, Laurel Realty
and Vice Chairman, Laurel Redevelopment Corporation*

I know of no one individual who has done more for Laurel and the surrounding community than Johnny Janosik. He loves to help people and his community and gives endlessly and unselfishly of his time, talents, and money to accomplish that goal. Most people have no idea just how much and how often Johnny has been there to help individuals, organizations, projects, and activities in our community because he does not seek recognition and praise for his good deeds. I feel that we are extremely fortunate and should be very proud to have Johnny as one of Laurel's most outstanding citizens and that he should be Laurel's "Citizen of the Year"—not just the year that he received that honor—but every year! Thanks again, Johnny, for all you have done and continue to do for the Laurel library and so many other causes. Laurel is a much better community because of you.

*Ed Ralph, President
Laurel Library Board of Commissioners*

Having lived in Europe, the Far East, and in many states in these United States, I have met some very memorable and outstanding people. But, it is in the little town of Laurel, Delaware, that I met my most memorable person of all: Johnny Janosik. While others at his time and stage of life retire to a quieter life, or at least a life disengaged from the everyday crowd, Johnny remains not only involved but in the center of the action. And, the "center of the action" in his case is dedicating his time and talents to the betterment of the people with whom he comes in contact. His overly generous philanthropic work, the Hope House Project, and the operation of Good Samaritan shop are mere examples of his dedication to helping others. His outstretched hand is offered to all irrespective of gender, social status, color or economic standing. His only criterion appears to be: do you need help? He is that rare bird, a human being who quietly dedicates his life on a day-by-day basis to helping others so they may have a better life. I consider it an honor to be associated with him.

*John Lopes, Senior Management Analyst
for the U.S. Department of Defense, Retired*

Foreword

Johnny Janosik remembers three things about growing up in the small, industrial town of Hopewell, Virginia: "I was always cold, hot, or hungry."

Now, over 60 years later, he looks back and can boast of overcoming these elements, along with a myriad of other challenges—obstacles that threatened to hinder his achievements. Johnny's respect is measured by his standing as one of the most significant and successful entrepreneurs in the state of Delaware.

Johnny Janosik has become a household name in communities throughout the eastern United States. The name is synonymous with high quality household furnishings; but more than that, it represents a standard of solid principles, strong values, and a good dose of common sense.

Some may think that "Johnny Janosik" is just a slogan concocted as an advertising gimmick. But Johnny Janosik is much more than a name hanging on the wall of a furniture empire. Johnny Janosik is an everyday person who represents the epitome of hard work, determination, commitment, and a downright savvy business sense.

Most important, Johnny Janosik represents hope. Yes, hope for people who need to believe that, although they are not blessed with high finances, intelligence honed by a college degree, or friends in high places, they too can be successful.

Johnny Janosik represents much more than furniture. Johnny Janosik represents a life philosophy that adheres to old-fashioned values like church, family and friends. This humble man serves as a shining role model—in a society often dominated by CEOs with a ruthless mentality and shark-like business ethics—that old-fashioned courtesy, compassion, and service are still the keys to success. Yet here, also, is a man whose success can be measured not only by the financial scale but by his willingness and desire to give back to his community and to others. Johnny Janosik spends many hours volunteering his time at the Good Samaritan shop, a local charity.

> "Johnny Janosik's basics are as easy as 1-2-3: **Be Honest, Be Fair, Give Good Service.**"

There he sits in a small corner office most mornings in the week, answering the phone and jotting down people's needs for help with food and clothing or medical, rent, and utility bills. More often than not, Johnny can be found talking to these people on the phone, helping them put their household needs into perspective, and sharing a plan to overcome the challenges that have become a part of their daily struggle. He identifies with these people because he once had to overcome these same life challenges himself.

Johnny does not abandon people in their time of need. Along with helping to provide immediate financial relief through the Good Samaritan shop, he has found jobs for some, provided vehicles and transportation for others, and helped deserving young people go to college. But Johnny does not view this as charity. He calls it "an investment" and believes that by helping others he is "paying life's tuition."

From his work with the Good Samaritan shop to his efforts in spearheading the building of Hope House, an emergency transitional housing project, Johnny Janosik has a keen sense of community. Each year, the Johnny Janosik business contributes thousands of dollars in furniture to a variety of charity needs, including families whose homes have been destroyed by fire and organizations that are addressing the plights of people in need.

Johnny Janosik lives and works by a simple philosophy. That philosophy involves what he calls going "back to the basics." What are these basics? In Johnny Janosik's words, "It's three fundamental ideals: *Be Honest, Be Fair,* and *Give Good Service.*"

Johnny Janosik may be small in physical stature, but he possesses a huge heart filled with sincere compassion. If the true measure of a man is his ability to make this world a better place through his presence, Johnny Janosik has not only met this measure but has also set the standard to which we should all aspire.

Tony E. Windsor

- Testimonials -

Johnny Janosik is a visionary. His vision, combined with the dedication of his wife, family and employees, has enabled him to be successful. His hard work and tenacity have allowed him to achieve his dream of being one of the largest and best retailers in the area.

Joanne Esham
Management, Johnny Janosik, Inc.

Johnny mirrors why my father came to this country for his American Dream. That being, America is the land of opportunity—if you work toward that dream. Johnny has earned the American Dream of success with his hard work, determination, resilience and perseverance. The words, "It can't be done," are not part of his vocabulary. He ventures where no man dares to go, dives in with all of his energy, and makes it work

Frank B. Calio Jr.
Delaware State Commissioner of Elections

I have known Johnny and Mary for nearly forty years now. For many years they were friendly competitors, and then I began working for them in 1995; now I am CEO for their company. Mary and Johnny have always had excellent work and business ethics. Most important, they care about their employees, their customers, and the community. They have worked hard all of their lives and have earned everything they have. There was never a free ride for them, and they never expected one. They began a small business that has grown to a nationally-recognized company with integrity and respect. I think that I am a better person for having worked with them, and I am always proud of working for them.

Frank L Gerardi Sr.
Chief Executive Officer, Johnny Janosik, Inc.

The principles of honesty, integrity, fairness and a strong work ethic are a way of life for Johnny. He is a true business professional and one who is living proof that if you take care of your customers and your employees they will take care of you. A man of vision, his civic leadership has led to prosperous and sensible growth in our community. Johnny's strong family values and deep sense of caring drive him to always be willing to offer a helping hand to those families in need and less fortunate. I am extremely proud and fortunate to know and work with Johnny and the Janosik family.

Betty Townsend
Senior Sales Manager, Johnny Janosik, Inc.

Chapter 1

STARTING AT THE BOTTOM

My father always said the only worker who starts at the top is a well digger. That's why I never had any preconceived notions about what it would take for me to get out of Hopewell, Virginia, and poverty. Looking back, I guess my mother and father raised my brother and sisters and me the best they knew how, even though their best never came close to the lessons that we learned from life itself.

Mom and Dad were no strangers to adversity. My father, John Phillip Janosik, was a second-generation immigrant from Czechoslovakia; my mother, Emily, who was of Polish descent, came to America from Russia. Coming to the United States meant everything to these simple people. Neither expected anything more than they were willing to earn, and they always recognized that the freedoms of this country are not free. My father was a hard worker. Though necessary in order to feed his family, Dad's work ethic provided less than a nurturing environment for my siblings and me.

My dad had a good vocation as a pipe fitter and knew his craft well. It certainly wasn't Dad's lack of skill or willingness to work that kept us wondering how we would find tomorrow's meal. It was the 1930s. Little by little, the industrial town of Hopewell, Virginia, began to bend under the weight of an economic depression. Finding work became just as much a part of Dad's job as the daily toil in the local silk mill. I guess I knew our family was in trouble when Dad followed work out of the country and ended up applying his trade in Brazil. His intentions were noble, but his absence in our three-room tar paper shack took its toll. Sure, he sent money home for the family; but with a third grade education, Mom simply lacked the ability to manage money properly.

Maybe it's not meant for an 11-year-old boy to become the "man of the house," but Mom needed help. She just couldn't handle the stress of managing a household with four kids while Dad was gone. I remember chopping wood, cutting grass and becoming extremely creative at finding food wherever I could. Hopewell was simply standing still in terms of its economy. The industrial mills were closing and laying off employees, and both money and food were scarce.

Newlywed John and Emily Janosik, Johnny's parents.

In addition to my chores at home, I recall hunting for squirrel and rabbit and selling them for anywhere between 10 cents and 25 cents apiece in the neighborhood. Believe me, to our neighbors the prospects of cooking up some fresh meat was exciting and worth every penny of the meager selling price. Looking back, I see this was my first and most memorable education in the retail philosophy of supply and demand.

Meanwhile back at home, while I was out hustling to find the next family meal, my older sister Mary was helping Mom take care of the house and raise the younger children. I guess as rough and rocky as our life was, we were able to maintain some semblance of a family structure.

Though the majority of my time was spent working to figure out how we could keep putting food on the table and hold the family together while Dad was gone, occasionally I was able to assume the role of a young boy. I kept up with my schoolwork while attending St. James Catholic School and even found time to play with the other kids in my neighborhood. With no such things as electronic gadgets or high-tech toys, we had to be creative and learn to entertain ourselves. The kids in our neighborhood really came together and worked as a team.

The way it worked was that one youngster would provide a baseball, another would bring a baseball glove, and then someone else would supply the baseball bat. Our play was far from sophisticated, but it worked, and we appreciated what we had. I recall playing baseball until the leather hide came off the ball. We would simply wrap the ball in tar tape and keep right on playing. It was fun. And in hard times, I guess it's more important than ever that kids get to have fun. Having those moments when we could escape the reality that we were poor and struggling meant everything. But it was what it was—temporary relief.

By the time my father returned home after about a year's absence and took a job at the Hercules Powder Plant, the family was crumbling under the strain. Mom and Dad tried to make things work, but by then the damage had been done. Eventually Mom and Dad split. My brother Billy and I stayed with Dad, while Mom moved away with Mary and my younger sister Evelyn. Having no telephone or dependable vehicle around the house, Billy and I were lucky to see our sisters and mother once a month. It seemed as if Mom just disappeared, taking a big hunk of our life with her.

But in times like that—even though we were young—we had to decide to either put up a futile fight against something we couldn't control, or pick up the pieces and try to build a future the best way we could. I knew my little brother needed me; and even though he would never admit it, so did my Dad. So I was determined to dig in and hang on for the fight. Life may have been hard, but it was certainly not impossible. It was just a matter of being willing to do what had to be done to survive. Little did I know then, but that lesson was destined to be a major part of my life's plan.

Over sixty years have passed since my childhood days in Hopewell. I find myself wondering where the time has gone. But standing outside in the parking lot of the Johnny Janosik furniture store complex answers that question pretty quickly. This has been an on-going, evolving business venture since my wife, Mary Louise, and I started working together back in 1953.

Today, even I am amazed by the growth of this family business. Looking up at the large sign that bears my name, I can't help but feel a certain degree of pride. But this is not an egotistical pride. It's a pride that stems from the fact that our business gives evidence to support what my father, mother, and grandparents believed when they came to the shores of America. They were confident that, no matter what their ethnic background or social and economic standing, they had the opportunity to be successful.

Being the product of a poor immigrant family makes me feel as though Johnny Janosik Furniture stands almost as a tribute and testimony to all that America has stood for in the eyes of the millions of immigrants who came to its shores seeking opportunity. So, no matter how much our country has suffered at the hands of those who choose to badmouth and criticize, she still reigns as the greatest country in the world and the true land of opportunity.

As strange as it may seem, starting as a young man with nothing in terms of finances has its advantages. It increases my gratitude. I'll always have something by which to compare my success and deeply appreciate what I have. I know that only by the grace of God can I enjoy the success that has been a part of this family business.

I only have to recall the days of my youth when we wondered whether there would be a meal on the table the next night. This may seem like a part of my life that would be best forgotten, certainly nothing reminiscent of the "good old days." Quite the contrary! I never want to forget those days of struggle and hardship because, along with the struggle came determination and perseverance that honed my skills for survival. No, I never want to forget those days. Above all, that memory keeps me humble. But, at the same time, it's made me strong. Through it all, I have not only survived but have learned that no obstacle is too hard to overcome. I've found that "when push comes to shove," I can push and shove with the best of them.

I guess to some my attitude may sound somewhat callous and cynical. I can't agree. This is just a philosophy that I adopted early in my life once I recognized that I wanted to plot my way in life as opposed to waiting to be handed a map telling me where I was going.

In Hopewell, Virginia, I watched as, one by one, members of my family lost their jobs and my brother and sisters quit school. I knew that without an education I would be setting myself up for failure and a reserved spot in the welfare line. I made up my mind then and there that this would not happen to me. If I were to change the forecast and build a life with more promise, I would probably have to do it somewhere other than Hopewell.

Johnny and his brother and sisters spent a great deal of recreational time with the kids in the neighborhood. Pictured here are the Janosiks with next door neighbors, the Goffs. The Goff family eventually moved to Sussex County, Delaware. This provided the catalyst for Johnny's move to Laurel, Delaware. Pictured are (left to right, front): Evelyn Janosik Brown, Bobby Goff and Billy Janosik; (left to right, back row): Mary Janosik Basil, Jack Goff, Ruth Goff, and Johnny Janosik.

Chapter 2

LEAVING POVERTY, HEADING FOR UNCERTAINTY

Mary and Pete Goff lived next door to my family while I was growing up in Hopewell. My brother, our sisters and I spent a lot of time hanging out with their children Jack, Bobby and Ruth. Miss Mary was a good friend of my mother, and the two always kept an eye out for trouble when we children tended to be up to no good.

Miss Mary and Mom were more than diligent disciplinarians; they were our guardians as well. I recall one day, when we were all out in the yard playing baseball, I found out just how important their guardianship could be to our welfare. Like most neighborhoods in America, we had our share of bullies. On this one day, a couple of bigger kids chose to pick on Jack Goff and me. The two of them knocked us down and were really whipping us. Suddenly, Mom and Miss Mary appeared out of nowhere. Miss Mary grabbed one of the boys and punched him straight in the face. The boys ran off, fearing for their lives. That memory will forever be one of the most treasured moments of my childhood days in Hopewell.

But just like our family, before long the Goffs met with the unfortunate realities of the industrial depression that gripped Hopewell. Pete Goff, a millwright by trade, learned of work up north where the industrial giant, DuPont, was building a nylon plant in Seaford, Delaware. As a matter of survival, the Goffs packed up and moved off to Delaware. Once again, I watched a part of my childhood dissolve as their car drove off into the distance.

The years proved to get no better, and my outlook did not improve. My older sister Mary quit school, followed eventually by my brother Billy. With one more year of high school ahead of me, I wanted desperately to make something of myself and to know what was going on in other parts of the United States. Certainly Hopewell did not represent the whole of the country's economic state.

We received an invitation from Pete and Miss Mary to visit them at their home in Laurel, Delaware. Plans took time, but eventually we loaded into Dad's 1937 Ford, equipped with a whopping 60-horsepower engine. We drove up U.S. 13 from Virginia and were almost stopped dead in our tracks by sudden gusts of wind.

After what seemed like an eternity, we arrived. Something about this little town called Laurel immediately struck a satisfying chord with me. The people seemed far friendlier than those we knew back in Hopewell. But, even more satisfying, there were jobs.

Laurel was a farming community. Unlike industrial towns like Hopewell, the farming communities produced a much-needed commodity—food. There were vegetable packing plants, restaurants, fertilizer plants, movie theaters and grocery stores, all apparently thriving. When we returned home following our visit with the Goffs, something told me I'd be back.

I did return the following year after I graduated from Hopewell High School. My friend Jack Goff was managing the Laurel Silco department store. He urged me to come to Laurel because truck farming was flourishing and the canneries were in full operation. He said if I did not get a job with one of the local canning houses, he would hire me at the Silco store.

So at the age of 16, standing five-feet six-inches tall and weighing 121 pounds, I boarded a snub-nosed Greyhound bus in early June of 1942 and headed north for Delaware. I cannot recall a time in my life when I was more scared. The bus held 16 to 20 passengers, and I was the only child on board. It was the first time I had ever left home alone, and I was indeed petrified. I spent the next few hours wondering if I had made a mistake.

We had a layover in Norfolk, just south of the ferry that crossed the Chesapeake Bay. I was horrified to learn that there were no buses heading out to Delaware until the next day. With just over $4 in my pocket, I had to find a room for the night. I was so scared I might somehow miss my bus that I wouldn't venture across the street for fear of getting lost. My room cost $1.90, so I was left to make my way to Delaware with about two dollars stuffed in my pocket.

Because I didn't know what was facing me over the next 24 hours, I skipped meals and only purchased a 10-cent soda in order to preserve the meager amount of money I was carrying. I went to my room and sat on the bed, and the panic in my heart led me to a point where I almost considered walking back home. Eventually I fell asleep. The next day I awoke and grabbed my duffle bag packed with all my worldly belongings, which I think included two pair of underwear, two pair of pants, and a shirt.

Once again, I boarded a bus and set out into the unknown. For the second leg of my journey, the bus drove onto the Little Creek/Cape Charles Ferry to cross the Chesapeake Bay. As we floated out into the gray, foam-capped waters, I suddenly feared we would somehow be lost at sea. I was so afraid that I stayed on the bus and wouldn't get out and walk around like the other passengers. Would this journey ever end?

Once on dry land, the bus started north on U.S. 13. In 1942 this was the main thoroughfare along the East Coast. Today that road is known as U.S. 13A, or the Old 13. A new multi-lane highway has since replaced it. In southern Delaware, however, north of the Maryland line, the Old 13 still runs into Laurel, along the same route I took 60 years ago.

I remember the bus stopping at every town from Virginia, through Maryland, and into Delaware. I was like the stereotypical child on a family trip (driving the bus driver almost mad) asking, "Are we there yet?" at each stop for fear I would miss my destination. As we got closer to Laurel, I recognized from

When Johnny came to Laurel, Delaware in 1942, he stepped off the Greyhound bus with $1.90 in his pocket. He went into Lowe's restaurant, located behind the Greyhound bus stop, and ordered a 10-cent soda from waitress Ermina Henry. Here Johnny visits with Ermina 60 years later.

10   Chapter 2 • Leaving Poverty, Heading for Uncertainty

our last visit the poplar trees that lined both sides of the highway like arches leading into town. Finally, after a day and a half of travel covering only 300 miles, we pulled into the Laurel Bus Stop on the corner of Central Avenue and Market Street.

I got off the bus with my bag and about two dollars. Behind the bus stop was a restaurant owned by a Mr. Lowe. I walked inside, and the first person I met was a waitress named Irmina Henry. I was starving but only ordered a 10-cent soda because I still didn't know what I'd be facing in the coming days. Miss Henry knew Mary Goff and pointed me toward her Market Street home, just two blocks away. Amazingly, 60 years later, Miss Mary still lives in the same house. At 95 years of age, she cuts her own grass; and just last year, I saw her up on a ladder painting her window ledges. She's a country girl from the hills of Virginia and one remarkable lady.

One of Johnny's favorite people is former Hopewell, Virginia, neighbor Mary Goff. Miss Mary and her family lived next door until moving to Laurel, Delaware, when the DuPont nylon plant opened in 1939. Mary's husband Pete, a millwright, moved to Delaware for employment. It was a short time later that Johnny accepted an invitation from the Goffs to visit them in their new home. This was the catalyst for Johnny's eventual move to Delaware.

I stayed with the Goffs during the summer of 1942. It was a summer that literally changed my life. After settling in, I took a job with Phillips Packing Company, which at the time was processing tomatoes trucked in from local farms. This was the first job I ever had that actually paid me money. I was making 25 cents an hour when I started, and by the end of the summer I was making 45 cents an hour. In all, during the summer of 1942, I had earned $92. I felt like a millionaire. It was truly the first money I ever had that I could call my own.

The summer came to a close, and I knew I had to return home to Hopewell. For some reason, Miss Mary said she knew that I would be back. She was right. I went home, and in only two weeks I decided that I had to get out of Hopewell and what was destined to be a bleak future. I guess my short stay in Laurel left a major impression on me. My work at the packing plant was hard, but it paid good money. And for the first time in my life, I knew what it felt like to walk around with money in my pocket.

I came back to Laurel in September 1942. This time, it was the trip that established me in what was to be my new home. Once again, I stayed with the Goffs, but that was short lived. I moved into a five-dollar-a-week boarding house on Poplar Street and took a job as an usher at The Waller Theater. Today, the former boarding house is the lodge home for Laurel's Independent Order of Odd Fellows.

Back in Hopewell, I graduated with only 11 years of school needed. In Laurel, schools required 12 years of classes. I was one year short and determined to get a high school diploma in Delaware because, after all, this was to be my home. So I walked into Laurel High School two weeks into the school year. I must have been pretty conspicuous because I only owned two pair of pants, and it was obvious that I lacked anything that even resembled stylish clothing. I was this short, skinny Slovak boy with the name Janosik, far from a hometown Laurel name. My survival instinct was truly tested there. Though I'm sure I would have had a hard time admitting it, I was actually up for the challenge.

Herman Kopp, the manager of the Waller Theater, was a good man who was in need of workers who were dedicated to the job. I was certainly committed to doing a good job at the theater but also had an interest in playing football for Laurel High School. I was skinny and fast and maneuvered well on the playing field. I convinced Mr. Kopp that I would not let my 3 p.m. to 6 p.m. football schedule interfere with my work at the movie theater. We had no night games back then because we had no lights for the football field. He was reluctant, but being an understanding man, he conceded to allow me to play football and keep my job. Though he was certainly fair and charitable toward me, I truly tested his patience when I also decided to play basketball for Laurel High School. This decision meant sports practice and games well into the night. I thought he would blow his stack. Then came warmer weather and baseball. I could throw a nice sinker, curve ball and slider, so I made the team as a pitcher. I thought Mr. Kopp would fire me for sure. But, as always, he adjusted to my schedule and kept me on at the theater. The truth is, if Mr. Kopp had given me an ultimatum, I would have had no choice but end my sports career. After all, the job paid $5 to $6 a week, and that was all that stood in the way of starvation and me.

Even as a teenager, I knew the value of making an honest living and being able to pay my own way. The job at The Waller Theater kept me in room and board. I had a good friend in Lee Riggin, my immediate supervisor at the theater. Lee, Don Bailey, Ethel Wheatley, Harold Culver and I made up the entire crew at the movie house. Harold helped me learn to run the projector, and Lee showed me how to change the marquis out in front of the theater. At night, when my shift would have normally ended, I'd take over for the projectionist and work until closing. I think, in hindsight, Lee saw my willingness to learn something new on the job as my desire to accept responsibility and move ahead. That's a quality I've always appreciated in my own employees.

During the summer following my graduation from Laurel High School, I took a job with C.C. Oliphant & Son as a sheet metal worker. I was employed there until I was drafted and went into the U.S. Navy.

Sixty years have come and gone since I made that trip out of Hopewell, Virginia, to Laurel, Delaware. A lot has changed since I worked at The Waller Theater. The main business complex for the Johnny Janosik furniture store sits on 30 acres of land along U.S. 13 south, just outside of the town corporate limits. Now with two locations in Dover and Laurel comprising 190,000 square feet of furniture showroom space and 220,000 square feet of warehouse inventory space, the family business has grown enormously. I'm proud that 300 employees depend on the Johnny Janosik store for their livelihood. That fact proves, even to me, that the drive to survive is a deep-seated characteristic.

Finding the courage to press on toward a goal like getting on a bus and going to a town that hardly makes a dot on a map can alter a person's entire life in a wonderfully positive way. If you've got an ounce of courage to look even your smallest fear in the face, then you've got a survival instinct. And it's one of those things that gets stronger the more you use it. Before you know it, you'll be able to confront your greatest fears.

I can attest to the saying, "What does not kill you makes you stronger." Let me tell you about World War II.

Chapter 3

THE SOUNDS OF GUNS AND WAR

Few things are more frightening than war. Since Vietnam, our country has been blessed with few major battlefields. The Persian Gulf War and our current defense against terrorism with *Operation Iraqi Freedom* have certainly put our brave military men and women in harm's way. I thank God, however, that thus far, America has seen nothing quite like the bloody carnage of World War II.

I can recall the tragedy and horror of this war effort firsthand. At 17, I was making some big decisions in my young life. I was aware that my brother Billy had quit school in Hopewell, Virginia, and joined the Navy. This was true to style for Billy. Even while we were young boys playing in the backyard, he demonstrated nothing less than a helter-skelter, devil-may-care attitude. Don't get me wrong. He was a good kid, just always full of mischief.

I suppose part of me wanted to join my brother in the military, but I wanted to get my high school education first. So I attended and graduated from Laurel High School before signing up for military duty. At the age of 18, it's safe to say most boys feel almost invincible. Though I knew from news accounts what was going on in both the European and Pacific Theater of the war, I was in no way prepared for the experience I was about to face.

The move from Hopewell, Virginia, to Laurel, Delaware, was the first time I'd ever been away from home by myself. As you know, I settled in Laurel. Even though I was only 16, I spent the next two years virtually on my own.

Now, my second trip away from familiar surroundings would take me not only out of state but also out of the country. It was September 1943. I was drafted by the United States military and headed off to Greenbay, Wisconsin, and the Great Lakes Naval Training Station.

Along with a bunch of other sailors, I boarded a train in Philadelphia that took us to Chicago and then on to Wisconsin.

Johnny Janosik entered the United States Navy in September 1943 during WWII.

I was scared to death. One man among the group had to be in charge of coordinating all the dining arrangements while on board the train. As fate would have it, I was chosen. This completely amazed me, considering other men in our group were old enough to be my father.

We were given funds to pay for three meals a day. Always the entrepreneur, I suddenly had a great idea. I realized that if we ate breakfast and skipped lunch, we could actually save money for the U.S. government off this deal.

Somehow, as brilliant as that idea seemed to me, the other sailors thought it was insane. I thought the rest of the men would hang me. I quickly learned that nothing, not even money, could stand between these men and their food.

As servicemen go, we were far from the cream of the crop. I suppose the well-to-do, educated men were back at college, leaving the war to be fought largely by miners, steel workers, and other working class men. We may not have been the best educated, refined group of people, but we all had one thing in common: we were going to fight and win this war!

Greenbay, Wisconsin, turned out to be, without a doubt, the coldest place on earth. Boot Camp will go down in history as probably my single-most extraordinary learning experience. I realized in quick succession that I was not there for a vacation. I had to buckle down and accept a load of discipline. Before I left the camp, I was thoroughly trained in how to take care of myself and keep things in proper order.

I think my key to success during basic training was having the proper attitude. I knew why I was there, simply did what I was told, and did not balk. It wasn't easy, but I felt then and still feel today that I learned valuable life skills during those weeks at Boot Camp. Each day that I exercised, drilled, and became totally exhausted was a day closer to why I was there—I wanted to get aboard a Navy ship.

I reaped my reward when I was finally assigned to the heavy cruiser, USS Louisville, which was undergoing an overhaul at the Naval base in Vallejo, California, near San Francisco. This ship was over 600 feet long and weighed in at over 13,000 tons.

I joined about 800 men who called this massive vessel home for the next two and a half years. Assigned to the "R" Division, which was short for the Repair Division, the Navy took note of my experience in welding and sheet metal work back in Laurel when I worked at C.C. Oliphant & Sons.

Our first stop was Pearl Harbor, Hawaii, where we did an extraordinary amount of practice drills with the big 8-inch guns. Over and over we loaded and shot those cannons. The whole ship rolled each time the rifles were discharged. This practice was necessary to assure that the ship would prove seaworthy during actual battle fire. After a month of intense practice, we were off for the tropics of the South Pacific—and hell.

We toured the entire Pacific over the next couple of years and the Marshall, Palaus, and Marianas Islands became my first

Johnny served over two years during World War II, assigned to the communications division aboard the USS Louisville.

exposure to the misery of war. Over and over, from the Battle of Leyte Gulf through Surigao Straights, Saipan, Tinian, and Guam, we encountered an enemy that I could never have dreamed up in my worst nightmare.

I'm proud to have been a part of the Navy interception of the Japanese Fleet at the Battle of Leyte Gulf. Our Seventh Fleet sank several battleships and cruisers. Historically, it's been determined that if it were not for our successful stand at Leyte Gulf, we could well have been defeated in the Philippines.

The Japanese were committed to this war far beyond what a normal human being could envision. Most of our soldiers just wanted to survive the guns, bombs, blood and gore that surrounded them on the Pacific Islands. But to the Japanese they were of no consequence. Death was the noblest thing that could happen while these men were fighting the western world. I actually watched not only Japanese soldiers but women and children commit suicide as, one by one, they leaped off cliffs during the invasion of Saipan and Tinian, their bodies floating in the water surrounding our ship. This memory still haunts me today.

One after another of our ships encountered Kamikaze pilots who, almost 60 years before our September 11, 2001, tragedy in New York, were flying fuel-filled airplanes into our ships in a militaristic frenzy. Hundreds of these Kamikaze pilots would fly in at a time. The goal was to strike as many of our ships as possible. They were looking for the bigger carrier ships because these would enable them to knock out a ship and airplanes, as well. We took three hits by these suicide bombers and had to head back to Pearl Harbor to undergo repairs. This overhaul at Pearl Harbor cost our involvement at Iwo Jima, one of the most famous battles of the Pacific Theater.

Even in the heat of WWII, I was searching for a way to turn a dollar. I was young but had never been one to stay out late at night and run to the bars. Most of my Navy buddies, on the other hand, found great pleasure in making liberty an extreme night of revelry. It occurred to me that my shipmates may want to look their best while out on the town, but few would take the time to make sure their Navy whites were pressed. I decided to buy an iron and ironing board and see if I had any takers. I was overwhelmed. I pressed uniforms for $1 each. In no time at all, I was making more money than the U.S. Navy ever paid me. My spirit of entrepreneurship was alive and well.

By the time the ship was once again ready for battle, I had transferred from the Repair Division to the Navigation and Communications Division. This transfer provided my first experience in radio repair, and my Navy experience in radio repair eventually led me to television repair work following the war. I was assigned to Radio 3, a six-foot by eight-foot transmitter room.

In June 1944, four other crew members and I were stationed in Radio 3 when a suicide bomber struck. The Kamikaze plane carried not only its fuel but a bomb, as well. The plane struck the ship's smokestack, directly behind one of the walls of Radio 3.

The impact blew a hole through the wall of Radio 3, and Bob Post and I were sure we'd been killed. He had his fingers blown off, and his face looked as if he'd been hit with a shotgun blast. The other three men were killed instantly. I scrambled down the ladder outside Radio 3 and was so scared I fell 20 feet to the deck below.

Lying side-by-side with others in the sick bay of the ship, I was told that the Radio 3 transmission room had taken a direct hit. The blast blew outward, devastating everything in its path. Fortunately, Bob Post and I were standing at the exact point of impact in the radio room. For that reason we were able to avoid being killed—kind of like being in the eye of a hurricane.

I was transported to a hospital ship and then on to a Naval hospital in Guam for about 30 days of recovery. In 1945 when the war ended, troops were beginning to be discharged and sent back to the states. I was among those who should have gotten to go home; but, because I was so young, they kept me aboard ship. This situation went on for eight months. Furthermore, our cruiser was converted into a troop ship, and we were sent all over the Pacific to pick up and transport soldiers who were on their way back to the states.

Thousands of soldiers were heading home, and we were well over capacity. We had soldiers sleeping on the decks or in any nook or cranny that could hold a sack. We always prided ourselves on keeping a clean, neat ship. But all that changed when we brought aboard the GIs. These were the "grunts" of the war. They were not used to having access to a shower,

Johnny aboard the Louisville during WWII.

and this attitude showed. We had learned to be conservative with our water on the ship, but not so with these Army soldiers. We were used to pulling the chain to open water for the shower just long enough to get wet; then we would soap down and pull the chain again to rinse off. The foot soldiers would get in the shower two at a time, and one would hold the water chain on continually while the other took a shower. We were always running out of water.

The GIs, who were used to sleeping in tents and foxholes near the battlefields, accused us of living in what they considered to be hotel accommodations. Traditional Army-Navy rivalry was thriving aboard the USS Louisville. I guess the fact that these guys were heading home made the situation a little more bearable for all of us.

Finally, after two and half years of service in the Pacific Ocean, my turn came to head home. Our ship left Pearl Harbor heading out of Honolulu for the Panama Canal and on to the Naval docks at Philadelphia. Once we arrived in Philadelphia, I worked for the next 30 days with crews as we moth-balled the ship, applying a cheesecloth and moisture-proof wax to protect the ship and its equipment.

We left Philadelphia in March of 1946 and traveled on to Bainbridge, Maryland, where I was finally able to make my trek back home to Laurel, Delaware. After military service, Uncle Sam gave us the option to become members of the 52/20 Club. This meant we could collect twenty dollars a week for 52 weeks.

Back in 1946, twenty dollars was a fair amount of money. Most jobs were paying about $25 a week, so a lot of the guys saw the military's offer as quite significant. Some men opted for this and just took a year off. Without question, we certainly deserved it. I, however, had no interest in the 52/20 Club.

After visiting family back in Hopewell, Virginia, I settled down in Laurel and applied the craft I had learned while in the service. I became an electronics technician for Osbourne Hudson, starting what would become a career in radio and television repair work.

I look back on my years in the service with pride. After almost 60 years, I'm of the notion that every young man at age 18 should do at least three years' service in the military. That may seem like somewhat unorthodox thinking to some, but I know what the military did for me.

I cannot find anything particularly positive about the death and destruction that almost became a way of life for me and the

Johnny spent almost three years service aboard the USS Louisville during WWII. He suffered serious injury in 1944 when the ship was struck by three Japanese Kamikaze planes.

thousands of other men who served our country. But I truly believe that if it weren't for my Navy career I wouldn't be where I am today. I was in a "do or die" survival situation on a daily basis, and it prepared me mentally and physically for the challenges that I've had to face throughout my life.

It's interesting to look back over my life and see how my experiences have knit together over the years to bring me to where I am today. If you're young and your destiny lies before you, be aware that it may well be the seemingly insignificant choices, a few major crossroads, and a wide variety of circumstances and opportunities that merge with your personality to define the person you will become.

Oh, another tip: Surround yourself with good people. They make all the difference.

Chapter 4

PLOTTING A COURSE – CHOOSING A PARTNER

*I*t would be nice to think that the success of Johnny Janosik Furniture is due exclusively to me. Pardon me for stifling a laugh behind my hand. I've been blessed with loyal employees and customers over the years, and a reliable staff is something every businessperson knows is a vital ingredient to a recipe for success.

But it's also important to provide an atmosphere that is conducive to promoting this type of loyalty. No matter how many ways I try to analyze how and why there is a Johnny Janosik business, I always come back to the roots of my heritage. The fact that I have lived poor and worked hard enables me to walk in the shoes of those determined, hard-working people that I am fortunate to call my employees.

My heritage demands that I pay the kind of fair, competitive wage that fosters the loyalty of good employees. At the same time, it's also my heritage that demands that employees be honest, trustworthy, and dedicated to their craft. All staff members, regardless of how menial or commonplace their responsibility, deserve recognition and deep appreciation. I trust I'll never be accused of looking down on any of my employees. That accusation would be ridiculous! I think many of them appreciate the fact that most of the jobs, especially in the warehouse operation, are ones I worked myself during the development of the business.

I'm amused to learn that some people who visit the furniture stores in Laurel and Dover, Delaware, actually think there is no real Johnny Janosik. They think this is simply a marketing logo. Then, when they see me at the store, they suspect I must be the grounds keeper. That's because I can often be found riding a lawn mower, watering flowers, or picking up trash in the parking lots. Plus, I don't fit the image of "dressing for success" when my traditional daily wardrobe consists of a cotton shirt, a pair of jeans, and sneakers.

But this is who I am. I'm not the kind of person that feels comfortable flashing around in a three-piece suit, wearing patent leather shoes. For me to dress in that type of attire would be dishonest. Besides, I don't want to wear

Pictured are newlyweds Johnny and Mary Louise Hedges Janosik. Johnny calls his wife his greatest friend and influence.

clothes that keep me worried that I'll spill something on my dress shirt, smear dirt on my sleeve, or dip my tie in the soup.

If you're ever looking for a poster child for "What You See Is What You Get," bring your camera my way. I believe in being honest both with other people and certainly with myself. Honesty is something that, regardless of income level, is affordable and never goes out of style. I think most people can pick up on someone who's a fake and lacks sincerity. It's a trait that seems to walk into a room ahead of them. I guess dressing as I do and speaking my mind are two ways I like to illustrate that I'll never lead someone to expect something of me that I'm not prepared to deliver.

Know what I enjoy most about our family business? It's that our philosophy is based on the sincere desire to be honest and provide true service, even beyond what the customer pays for. People want to feel they get their money's worth in any purchase. I think many businesses fail because they don't provide something more than the customer buys. This idea doesn't mean a business has to give away the profits. It does mean that we, as businesspeople, should be just as interested in making sure consumers get good service as they do a quality product. It's not only satisfying to know that we're providing service that goes beyond simply helping someone load the mirror into his or her trunk—it's also good business.

As businesspeople, we want to set the kind of tone that makes people want to come back and visit us again, whether they buy anything or not. This philosophy is a matter of being responsive to the customer not just during the sale but, more important, after a product has been delivered to the home. To determine what constitutes good service, we only need to ask ourselves one thing: What we would like to experience when making a purchase?

I admit that I've always had a vision for recognizing business trends and creating ways to stay on top of the cash flow. These are certainly important to any business. I think, however, I would be totally remiss not to cite the old cliché, "Behind every successful man is a good woman." This adage is certainly true in my case. The only adjustment I'd make in this is the fact that Mary Louise has never been "behind me." She's always been right there beside me. I've been blessed with a wife and partner who not only puts up with the sometimes pragmatic and most times overwhelming person known as Johnny Janosik but who has, over the years, stood as the cohesive bond that keeps our family and business together and healthy.

I tend to run off in a thousand directions, trying to champion a wide variety of projects in the scope of a month's time. Mary Louise says I start projects and then leave them for her to take care of while I move on to another challenge. I can't argue with that observation.

I think the first time I met my future wife will always be fixed in my mind. I was 23 years old, fresh out of Valparaiso Technical Institute in Indiana, where I studied electronic engineering and specialized in television repair. I came back to Laurel, Delaware, and went to work at Osbourne Hudson's television service store as a TV repairman. On Fridays and Saturdays until 9 p.m., the store transformed into a record shop, and I spent extra shifts working at the store.

I was friends with a fellow we called "Skinny" Stoeckels. Skinny's friend was also a friend of Mary Louise Hedges. I knew the Hedges family. Actually, a few years before, I was pretty good friends with Mary Louise's brother. They were a hard-working farming family who enjoyed a wonderful reputation in the community.

Mary Louise would come into the record store where Skinny and his friend, Sue Parham, worked. Mary Louise was the kind of girl who always seemed to be laughing and giggling about something or another. Skinny told me I should ask her out on a date, so on this one particular evening, I decided I would. To my amazement and embarrassment, when I asked her out, Mary Louise laughed and took off running out of the store.

I was devastated. No, actually I was insulted. I went next door to Bill North's Restaurant and sat drinking a soda and pouting. I could hardly imagine that here I was, a bona fide college graduate, giving a 17-year-old high school girl the opportunity and privilege of my company, and she left me standing there like a fool.

But not for long. A little while later, Mary Louise came back to the restaurant and explained that she thought I was joking when I asked her to go out on a date. She said she thought that because I was 23 years old and she was only 17 I would consider her too young. I felt a great relief after that explanation, and I wasted no time in scheduling our first date.

I've always prided myself on being able to size up a situation and make a quick and accurate decision. That's how I've always operated my business. I don't like to spend a lot of time pondering and wondering because, most likely, something else will come along tomorrow that will need my attention, so it suits me best to think diligently but quickly.

That's exactly what happened during my first date with Mary Louise. I determined that she was the woman I not only wanted to make a life with but needed to, as well. I saw her as a very serious person who knew what she wanted. She was already making plans to attend nursing school after graduation.

I remember actually telling Mary Louise after our first date that I was not sure how she felt, but I was ready to get serious. As I said earlier, I knew her family and you can often tell what kind of a person someone is based on his or her family. I knew that Mary Louise came from a good family, and I believed that she would be good for me. I could not have been more correct.

Not only did I fall in love with Mary Louise, but I fell for her mother, too. I suppose that deserves an explanation. Back in 1949 when we started dating, I played baseball with the Sharptown, Maryland, Central Shore Baseball League. A ritual with the league was to practice every Saturday and play ball every Sunday. Mary Louise hated baseball, but she would travel to my games every Sunday. Before the season was over, she loved the game.

Well, along with the weekend baseball ritual, there were the traditional Sunday dinners cooked and served by Mary Louise's mother, Lulu Hedges. A home-cooked meal to me was more of a luxury item; it just never happened at my house. Lulu was an outstanding cook, and I was a real fan of her Sunday dinners. Plus, she and I hit it off right from the start. As a matter of fact, I think Mary

Louise began to question whether it was her or Lulu's company and cooking that kept me around.

Looking back, I think it was the absence of my mother in my childhood home that created such a special maternal appreciation for older women. I guess I just felt comfortable and enjoyed the pleasant exchanges with someone like Lulu who helped me recapture the mother-son relationship that had been taken from me at the age of 11.

My wife and I have celebrated over 50 years of marriage. We have three beautiful daughters: Linda Kaye, Christina Maria, and Lori Ann, all of whom have blessed us with beautiful grandchildren. At one time or another, all three of our daughters have been a part of the Janosik family business, but today only Lori Ann remains actively involved.

With two Delaware locations and over $40 million dollars a year in sales, it's safe to say that the business is doing well. Mary Louise is the company CEO, and even though neither of us draws a paycheck from the business, we remain an active part of the day-to-day operations.

A lot has happened since I stood in the record shop at Osbourne Hudson's

While Johnny was "courting" his future bride, Mary Louise Hedges, the two traveled in Johnny's 1949 Ford.

store and asked Mary Louise for a date. Time has changed a lot of things. I'm sure we would both admit to moving a little slower and tiring a bit quicker. But one thing that time has actually made stronger over the years is our faith—a faith that after only one date led us to believe that ours was a love that was destined to last and make us both better people because of it.

As it turns out, we would need both faith and love to make it through the coming years. Let's take a closer look at this work ethic of mine and Mary Louise's reaction to it as we step back in time—to the days of television tubes and flickering hopes.

Chapter 5

MEETING CHALLENGES, FACING ADVERSITIES

A survivor, that's what I've always considered myself to be—with regard to economic endurance and my personal well-being, alike. As with many people, I've had my share of hardships and troubles over the years. But, as you might have guessed, what didn't kill me made me stronger.

My early professional career suffered many adversities, but each allowed me to grow in some way. For instance, in the early 1950s, I'd been working for the RCA Service Company in Easton, Maryland, as a service technician for three years when the economic forecast turned sour. I could see the future looked gloomy for the nationally-recognized television pioneer.

I started working for the RCA Service Company not long after graduating from Valparaiso Technical Institute. The money was great, about $100 a week. RCA had developed the black and white television and was tops in the market. But soon, competition started moving in with other models of black and white televisions. The televisions were cheaper and not necessarily better. Price drives the marketplace, however, and eventually RCA found themselves selling the highest-priced brand of television. So RCA started slowing production and I relocated to Easton, Maryland. Then, over the next couple of years, RCA began closing many of its service operations, and I moved to their Salisbury, Maryland, location.

By 1953, I knew that the economic forecast was not good and it wouldn't be long before RCA would be out of the local area with its service operations. What at face value seemed to be a career disaster was something that I was able to convert into one of the most significant and prosperous moves of my professional career.

My survival instinct kicked in, telling me that I should give my two weeks' notice and strike out on my own before the service company closed altogether. With RCA service companies closing in the southern Maryland/Delaware region, the field was wide open for a hard-working television technician. I theorized that within five years of starting to work with the RCA Service Company, I would have my own business. I was wrong. I had my own business in just three years.

The nice thing about working for a large company like RCA is that, because the organization tends to diversify, its technicians are cross-trained in a variety of areas. I only worked for RCA three years; but, during that time, I received training for not only electronics but also for servicing window air conditioners and appliances. When a service technician went out on call, the truck was equipped with whatever it took to get the job done—whether a television, antenna, air conditioner, or refrigerator.

When the RCA Service Company closed, television dealerships were in dire need of technicians to service their products. I teamed up with another former RCA television technician, Marion "Reds" Payne, and started a business called Mobile TV. I operated the business out of the basement of my home on U.S. 13A, just south of Laurel. The business did service work throughout southern Maryland and Delaware and stayed fantastically busy.

By 1955, I was completely overwhelmed with work, much more than I could realistically handle. One day, a former RCA Service Company manager, Bob Barnes, showed up on my doorstep. A few years earlier, Bob had been transferred from the Easton, Maryland, location to a branch near Atlantic City, New Jersey.

He said he wanted to get back to work in the local area because he was tired of the commute to New Jersey. I knew Bob to be an extraordinary manager and was elated to have him on board. He wanted a partnership, so we entered into an agreement. The cost was $3,000 each, and we moved to Salisbury, Maryland, where we rented a larger shop in hopes of increased growth.

The business remained Mobile TV, and we were extremely successful. We did home service work for 21 dealerships, covering an area throughout the lower Eastern Shore of Maryland and Delaware. We accumulated 13 service men doing six to 20 service calls a day in a 50-mile radius.

> "I teamed up . . . and studied ways to use my knowledge."

Once again, I studied ways to use my knowledge as an electronic technician and used my knack for entrepreneurship to identify new opportunities. As I visited the dealerships that we were doing service work for, I found that most of them were taking used television sets as trade-ins on new sets. The used television sets were piling up at these dealerships, and I asked if I could have them. Eager to get them out of their way, the dealers gladly turned them over to me. Pretty soon my living room was filled with used televisions. Having picked RCA's brain while I worked there, I was able to find the parts and refurbish them. Sometimes I'd have no more than $5 in parts, and I could sell the repaired sets for between $50 and $100. People in those days had a hard enough time purchasing a new television set, much less getting a second one. But my side business made it financially feasible for people who didn't have a television to get one or, in other cases, to purchase a second set. I was living in Salisbury at the time and the used television business became a lucrative side opportunity for me. This is a perfect example of how one man's trash can literally become another man's treasure.

I always knew I wanted to take my work back to Laurel. My opportunity came in 1958. Bob came to me and said he felt the business was about to go through a slowdown in work. He wanted to go on his own and asked if we could reach an agreement. I opted to buy him out of half the business, and he let it go for $5,000. I had saved $2,000, so I visited my old friend Harold Smith at Sussex Trust Bank in Laurel. I borrowed the $3,000 I needed for the balance of the buyout and had it paid back within a year.

After two years, we hit the Eisenhower recession. I decided that paying utilities and rent at the Salisbury shop was not a wise investment of my hard-earned dollars, so I made arrangements to move from Salisbury into a home I had built on Allen Avenue in Laurel. The home had a nice basement, so it immediately became my office. I changed the business name to "Johnny's TV" and continued to do television repair work in homes. Mary Louise answered the telephone and kept the books for the operation. And that's how our family business got started in 1953.

I look back over the early days with fond recollection; however, they were not without some harrowing and uncomfortable experiences. Being a television repairman was not always simply repairing the inner workings of a television set. It also involved such duties as erecting and repairing television antennas that sometimes towered 40 feet in the air.

I recall one such experience while I had my service repair business on U.S. 13A. I traveled with my assistant, "Reds" Payne, the first person I ever employed, to Seaford to take down a 40-foot telescoping pipe antenna that stood at the side of a home. I'll never forget the 6,400-volt high-voltage line that ran through the tall pine trees that surrounded the house.

We decided to cut all the guide wires that were used to support the antenna and then push the antenna down between the rows of trees. It didn't matter what condition the old antenna was in by the time we were done because we were there to install a new antenna. Basically, the old one was nothing more than junk to be hauled away from the site.

I told Reds to hold the base of the antenna while I was up on the peak of the roof cutting the last two guide wires. Once the wires were cut, I pushed the antenna and suddenly saw what appeared to be something akin to a welder's arc. The antenna was literally melting into its concrete base. Sparks were flying, and I quickly realized that we had pushed the antenna into the transmission line that fed local electric service to the house. If both Reds and I had not let go of the antenna so quickly after pushing it down, we would have been electrocuted.

I was on the roof at this point, panicking, when the woman who lived in the house came running out into the yard screaming that her house was on fire. By now, curious neighborhood kids had shown up on the scene, and it was fast becoming a circus—a very dangerous circus, but a circus nonetheless.

I knew then that the power lines were keeping the antenna charged, and it was connected directly to the house, creating an arc. My panic intensified. I knew that somebody had to get into the house to find how to cut the electric power. In my state of panic, I leaped from the roof and shattered my foot. This did not stop me, however, as I continued into the house.

Limping full-speed into the kitchen, I was greeted by flames shooting up from behind the stove. I moved the stove and found that the copper gas line had been severed from the force of the electric charge and was now flaming like the end of a blowtorch. I asked where the gas main was, and the woman told me it was behind the house. I didn't even look for a door. I threw open a window and jumped out into the backyard. I found the gas turn-off valve and cut the gas supply into the house. Immediately, the flames went out at the end of the gas line in the kitchen.

But now I had to find the main fuse box to cut off the power in the house. The woman said the box was located in the garage. I frantically searched the garage but found nothing resembling a fuse box. Suddenly, I saw bare wires hanging from the wall. On the other side of the garage lay the fuse box. The arc created by the antenna falling on the power lines allowed the full impact of the 6,400-volt power to charge into the fuse box through the 220-volt line. This created a power burst that literally blew the fuse box off the wall with the impact of a bomb.

By now the Seaford Volunteer Fire Department had arrived on the scene with four trucks and 30 men, joined quickly by the power company who cut off electric service to the entire east side of the city. Everything was now under control, and no one was hurt—unless you count my injured foot from the jump from the roof and, of course, my pride. At that point I wanted to crawl into a hole.

The family was very understanding. As we were cleaning up the mess around the house, my foot really began to throb. Someone suggested I go into the bathroom and clean up and perhaps I would feel better. So I went into the bathroom and turned the water on at the sink and began to wash my face and hands. I did feel a little better, but that feeling was short lived, as I began to feel water pouring onto my feet. I looked down and found no drainpipe under the sink. Looking up at the ceiling and wall, I saw that the light fixture was blown out; and a soot trail indicated that the electric charge had apparently run down the line along the wall and grounded at the drainpipe, completely melting it. I had a feeling this was one nightmare that was never going to end.

Amazingly, I was actually able to get through that ordeal with no one getting hurt. The power company only charged me about $168 to fix the wiring, and the household insurance covered the interior repair work.

I got home that evening and then my foot really started to ache. My family physician, Dr. Joe Elliott, came over to take a look and found it was, in fact, broken. The next day he put a cast on it, and I told him that there was no way I could miss any work because I had a backlog of service calls and was working for myself.

I limped around the next day, creating a severe problem with my toe that was unbearable, to the point of not being able to walk or do any work. Dr. Elliott came back over to my house and put a small brown stub on the end of the cast near the heel, so I was able to make my way around. That turned out to be the only day I missed from work during the entire ordeal.

Not all my misfortunes occurred on the job. I remember a 1958 station wagon that had less than 400 miles on its odometer. Mary Louise and I and two of our close friends, Dean and Dusty Betts, were heading home from a night out in Dewey Beach, Delaware.

Mary Louise was driving, and as we headed west on Route 9 toward home, I saw the glare of headlights coming directly toward us. I realized that Mary felt confident she was in the correct driving lane and had no intention of veering out of the way of the oncoming vehicle. Seeing no alternative to certain disaster, I grabbed the steering wheel and ran our brand new car into a ditch. The oncoming vehicle never realized it was in the wrong lane and subsequently struck the left back quarter panel of our car. Though sufficiently shaken, all four of us, as well as the driver of the oncoming vehicle, were physically fine.

But now I was short one service vehicle for Johnny's TV. The next day I went to a Seaford, Delaware, automobile dealership and bought another 1958 station wagon. I was able to have my car repaired by my insurance company and get the new station wagon for only $400 difference. I was back in business!

But, as fate would have it, my good fortune didn't last long. In late summer of 1958, I was traveling to Harrington, Delaware, to look at a swimming pool I was thinking about installing at home. I was driving along U.S. 13, north of Seaford near the Redden turnoff. It was about 8:30 a.m., and I was about to cross in front of the intersection when I saw a tractor-trailer loaded with chickens coming onto the highway, totally oblivious to the stop sign because the driver was stone cold asleep!

I remember vividly looking at the speedometer on my car's dashboard, and it read 57 miles per hour. There were no seat belts in those days, so realizing I would be making certain contact in short order, I locked the brakes and turned my wheel to the left and struck the tractor-trailer truck near the second set of rear-end tractor wheels. I shoved my arm through my steering wheel to hold myself. The impact of the collision threw me out of the car, through the windshield, and then pushed me back into the car again.

The tractor-trailer dragged my car down the right-hand lane, across the intersection, and then across the southbound lane where it stopped near a telephone pole. Completely dazed, I stumbled out of the car and fell into the grass at the side of the road where I lay until Delaware State Police Officer, Eugene Womack, showed up. I remember it was Eugene because we both graduated from Laurel High School. A second state trooper, Jack Short, also a good friend of mine, also arrived on the scene. Jack said that the truck driver remembered his traveling speed to be 60 miles per hour when he fell asleep at the wheel. Given my speed of 57 miles per hour, Jack estimated that we had about 3,000 pounds of weight on impact. With my arm locked inside the steering wheel on impact, I was lucky to still have the arm.

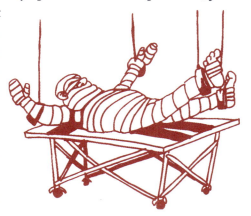

I also recall having about 400 television tubes in the back of my station wagon that were now covering the

Chapter 5 • *Meeting Challenges, Facing Adversities*

entire length of the roadway. My devoted brother-in-law, Nate Hedges, came to the accident scene and gathered up all the tubes from the road.

I was transported to Nanticoke Memorial Hospital in Seaford, where I was treated for three broken ribs, three chipped vertebrae, and a crushed arm. I lay in the hospital emergency room, my face covered with glass, which came from going through the windshield of my car.

The nurses were trying desperately to get the tiny slivers of glass off my face without either cutting my face or getting them in my eyes. In a few minutes my wife showed up at the hospital. Her first reaction upon seeing me lying in the treatment room was to ask, "What have you done now?" This seemed to become Mary Louise's stock response to my many accidents and one that seemed to lack an authentic ring of sympathy. As a matter of fact, this trite greeting reflected Mary's belief that I had a magnetic attraction to accidents.

Johnny has faced and overcome many challenges throughout his life, including medical emergencies. Pictured here is the aftermath of a 1958 motor vehicle accident in which his 1958 station wagon collided with a tractor-trailer truck along US 13 near Redden Road.

Seeing that the nurses were having difficulty getting the tiny, powdery pieces of windshield glass off my face, Mary Louise made what I felt was a very astute suggestion. She recommended they use the sticky side of duct tape, wrap it around their hands and then pat over the glass to remove it from my face. The nurses immediately tried this suggestion and, sure enough, it worked!

I remained in the hospital for the next 21 days. It was mid-August, and we were experiencing a heat wave. The hospital had no air conditioning at that time, so my recovery was far from comfortable.

Only a couple of years after this harrowing experience, once again, I managed to attract the attention of the invisible accident magnet. In the early 1960s, I was working at my shop on Market Street in downtown Laurel. I was caught up on service calls, so I decided to paint the windows and trim of our two-story building. Another service man, Gil Clemens, agreed to help me with the painting.

I had a ladder propped against the back of the building, which led from the blacktop pavement up to where I was doing some trim work around the upstairs apartment windows. I recall that all seemed fine, and then I reached to dip my brush in the paint. Suddenly the ladder slipped from under me, and I was thrown to the pavement some 20 feet below. I struck my head and was knocked unconscious. To all who witnessed the event, however, it seemed as though I had killed myself. I was loaded into the Laurel Volunteer Fire Department ambulance and rushed to the all-too-familiar Nanticoke Memorial Hospital.

Dr. Joe Elliott treated me at the hospital and said that I had come closer to death during this incident than when I was involved in the major traffic accident a few years earlier. This was because I split my head open in the fall from the ladder. I also broke my collarbone.

I was lying in the treatment room, my head throbbing from the impact. Suddenly, I caught sight of her in the corner of my eye—Mary Louise heading down the hall toward my room. As she made her way up to me, finger waving in my face, I knew she was about to once again utter those familiar words, "What have you done now?" I cut her off at the pass when I looked up at her and simply said, "If you open your mouth and say one word, I'll hit you right in the teeth."

Needless to say, my words of light-hearted warning left Mary Louise speechless. They also lightened the room as nurses and even Mary burst out laughing. I just don't think I could have given Mary any more support for her theory that I was somewhat less than nimble or cautious, even though I knew she was correct in her observation.

The really sad ending to this particular incident came after I got out of the hospital. Unable to complete the work of painting the back of the store because of my sudden disability, a local painter, "Raz" Horstman, offered to finish the work. He charged me $85 to do the entire job, including windows and trim.

I was trying to save money by doing the job myself and was almost killed; plus I ended up costing the business from my time off with hospitalization and recovery. I would have saved a lot more money, time, and physical trauma if I had simply hired Raz to do the job to begin with. Oh well, this is one of those times when I had to believe there was a lesson in there somewhere.

My whole experience in life and business has been a roller coaster of ups and downs. Fortunately, I always had somebody next to me to help me hang on.

Chapter 6

DON'T FORGET WHO BRUNG YOU TO THE DANCE

*T*he relationship I have with Mary Louise is as much a partnership as a marriage. I've always considered myself to be a visionary. I have a knack for assessing where we are at any given time in reference to the business, then recognizing where we need to be. Then it's a matter of plotting a course of action to get there. Mary Louise is the one who carries out the plan in the day-to-day operations. It's a team effort.

This team concept spills over into the overall operations of Johnny Janosik Furniture because the employees share our enthusiasm and desire for making sure the business stays customer-driven.

There's an old saying that I like to keep in mind: "Don't forget who brung you to the dance." I'm sometimes in awe myself at the success of the business. That success is due, however, not only to the business vision of the Janosik family but also to a strong commitment from our employees to be consumer oriented.

In the June 2002 issue of *Furniture Today*, a national industry trade magazine, Johnny Janosik was listed as one of the top 151 furniture stores in the country in terms of growth. At the same time, the store was also honored with a plaque naming us number eight in the country in Lazy Boy gallery sales.

Johnny Janosik averages retail sales in excess of $40 million a year. Friday through Sunday alone will produce half a million dollars in sales. I never dreamed that our vision would reach this level.

Success of this magnitude can easily contribute to a sense of egotism. For this reason I always remember that I didn't come to the dance alone. It's the hard work of family and employees and the loyalty of our customers that 'brung" Johnny Janosik to the dance. So, above all else, it's essential that the business stay consumer-oriented and friendly in all it does while offering a comfortable, rewarding work environment for our employees.

> "The real lessons of life come when you're striving to make ends meet."

I'm proud that our family business has been able to contribute to the area economy because, after all, this has been home for my family and me for the past 60 years. The hustle and bustle of the retail business often makes it difficult to remember that there was a time when my only contribution to the town of Laurel was ushering people in and out of the movies at The Waller Theater down on Central Avenue when I was 17 years old.

But I guess the real lessons of life come while you're striving to make ends meet. I can recall a time when, after almost two decades of running a television and appliance business in downtown Laurel, Mary Louise and I realized that in order to keep the business healthy, we'd have to get out to the highway for more visibility and room to expand.

Some people felt we were abandoning the town of Laurel by considering a move out to the highway, even though it was less than two miles away. It was, however, a survival move for the business, plain and simple. We had outgrown our downtown location, and it was becoming more and more difficult to pull motorists off the highway and bring them to the downtown district to investigate shopping opportunities.

In 1977, within six months, our downtown business went from 11 employees and sales of $900,000, down to six employees and sales of $300,000. We were going broke fast. Thomas R. Young, a friend of mine who was also in the appliance business, offered me an opportunity to help offset my losses at the store by helping him with deliveries. He told me that it was furniture that would hold the key to future success, not appliances. He had added furniture to his appliance dealership and encouraged me to do the same.

Like many other communities in America during the mid-1970s, Laurel was experiencing death in its once-thriving downtown area. One by one, businesses were moving out to U.S. 13, where much more visibility and a high-volume of traffic abounded.

This situation was hard, however, for those of us who seemed to be leading the exodus. We were labeled as almost traitors because we seemed to be turning our backs on the town's economy for the lure of the busy highway. True, we were seeking opportunities that the heavily traveled highway could bring our business, but in no way were we turning our backs on our community.

In the spring of 1978, the evidence was clear, and the verdict was ours to decide. We could either stay in the restricted confines of our Market Street business location and die with the rest of the downtown area, or we could migrate to U.S. 13 and gain the much-needed visibility.

I drove up and down a 20-mile strip of U.S. 13, hoping to find a piece of property for sale that would meet our business needs. I happened to have a conversation with a friend of mine who also opened a business on the highway. Bob Hickman, a successful local developer made me aware that a 21-acre parcel of property was for sale adjacent to his RV sales lot.

One morning, Bob took me to the property. It was literally a 30-foot by 440-foot chicken house standing in the middle of a cornfield. The property owner was using the chicken house to board horses. The selling price was $64,000.

As you know, I don't waste a lot of time making decisions. By that afternoon, I decided I wanted to buy the chicken house. The downtown business had several upstairs apartments and I had developed at least $125,000 in equity. The bank was happy to make the loan; and within the next couple of days, I owned a chicken house and a cornfield.

I remember well the odor that hit me when I walked into the chicken house for the first time. It had been home to a number of horses, and the smell that lingered in the air was clear evidence of this.

We stripped the inside of the chicken house, and I cleaned the entire building with a chemical called Chlordane, a chemical so strong that it's even illegal to use it today. I decided to leave the horse stalls in the chicken house and, once successfully cleaned, the TVs, appliances, and furniture were brought in. By the end of 1978, we had $1 million in sales.

After many years of selling televisions and appliances, I followed Tom Young's advice, and we now included furniture in our store inventory. Furniture proved to be the foundation for our success. We were closing out the 1970s with extraordinary success. But the economy was about to show us that it still held all the cards to determine whether we would continue to enjoy that success.

The 1980s came, and within the first year our country experienced a recession. Perhaps for the rest of the nation it was a recession; however, for us it was almost a dead stop. Our $1 million-a-year business was screeching to a halt. Nothing was moving off the sales floor.

I was 54 years old, and the business had hit rock bottom. The store inventory was not moving; however, rent, payroll and bank loans all still came due. I had to do something to keep us from going bankrupt. Although I was always the astute visionary, my vision had become blurred. For the first time in almost 25 years, I wasn't sure what I was going to do.

I've always heard that "when the going gets tough, the tough get going." This attitude is the secret to why I launch into survival mode when faced with financial challenges. This situation wasn't just about my financial future; I had a family and employees depending on the success of the business.

I almost laugh when I think about the things I did over the next couple of years to keep the business afloat. It was 1981, and I learned about a growing interest across the country in wood stoves. The economy had gotten so bad that people were trying to conserve any way they could. This included fuel conservation.

So I became a Black Bart wood stove distributor. My knowledge of the appliance business allowed me to have contacts with dealers throughout the region. I found 10 dealers who were interested in stocking wood stoves.

The wood stoves moved fast. I bought them 100 at a time and drove five days a week delivering wood stoves to dealers in Delaware, Maryland, Pennsylvania, and New Jersey. Within a year we had sold 3,000 wood stoves.

Interestingly enough, wood stoves sold in the cities with no adequate wood supplies. So I bought a truck with a 24-foot body. I used a chain saw and, with the help of my store employees, cut wood on our property, loaded it, and hauled it to New York where I sold it for firewood.

Before long, modern-day people found the wood stoves too dirty and hard to clean inside their homes. The wood stove frenzy wore off. Then kerosene heaters became the rage. I was right there waiting. As quick as the tide of consumer interest shifted, I sold kerosene heaters to the dealerships.

The summer of 1981, since I had invested in the truck, I decided to put it to good use. While it wasn't the season for wood stoves or kerosene heaters, produce is a major industry in Laurel, Delaware, and activity at the local auction block during the summer is phenomenal. Some of the sweetest and most beautiful watermelons and cantaloupes in the country come through Laurel's Watermelon Auction block.

So as another business venture, I loaded my truck with watermelons and delivered them to major supermarkets in the Washington, D.C. and Baltimore areas.

I did this as a matter of survival. I didn't consider watermelons, wood stoves, or kerosene heaters to be my specialty, but they kept the business running and the employees paid.

The early 1980s took my survival skills to a new level. I was selling TVs, appliances, carpet, and furniture at Johnny Janosik's store. But I knew change was coming. The commercial identity of the area was changing, and major chains like Lowe's were moving in.

Johnny Janosik's TV and Appliance store had earned the reputation of being the biggest Whirlpool and RCA dealership on the Eastern Shore. But I knew that with the major chains coming into the region, I couldn't keep up competitively.

Television sales had already been taken out of the business. Within a year, we got out of appliances; soon afterward, our carpet center was gone, too. We had finally found our business niche; it was furniture, bedding, and accessories.

Interestingly enough, lying just a short distance from where our new furniture store had been developed, twelve acres of land sat barren (part of the original parcel of land that I purchased on the highway). Little did I realize that this, like a hidden oil field, would provide a catalyst for extreme growth in the Johnny Janosik business.

I had a number of ideas about how to subdivide the 12-acre tract into several business opportunities that could be developed. No businesspeople in the area, however, would bite. During a trip to Florida one year, Mary and I undertook a quest for antiques. We stopped at every flea market between Delaware and Florida. While we were walking through a huge indoor flea market in Daytona

Beach, Florida, an idea struck me. Why not bring this concept to Laurel?

I went home and began planning. Within a few months, the U.S. 13 Outlet Market was standing on the twelve acres that had previously been vacant. Built with the same design as our furniture store, the indoor flea market looked like a large chicken house. The business caught on like wildfire. We filled the building with vendors, and it became a regular attraction for locals as well as people from all over the East Coast who traveled busy U.S. 13.

I had no intentions of selling this business because it was bringing in $600,000 a year after taxes to the Janosik enterprise. I had enough sense, however, to sit down and listen when a developer who liked the concept of the indoor flea market approached me. I met with my accountant and decided that, because the business was doing so well, I would take no less than $2.1 million. After working details out with the bank, the sale was completed. A local realtor by the name of Herb Dayton handled the sale for Cooper Realty; and, though early in his real estate career, he walked away with $100,000 commission. The news hit all the local press.

This kind of occurrence makes me appreciate the opportunity we have here in the United States to practice free enterprise and entrepreneurship. Here was a business that I had not even considered while developing the U.S. 13 property for the Johnny Janosik furniture store; yet it turned out to be the rocket that shot the Johnny Janosik business to a new level. After making the $2.1 million sale and covering the $500,000 I had in construction costs and Uncle Sam's share of $500,000, I walked away with a clear $1.1 million.

I've tried to pass my work ethic and entrepreneurship on to my children and grandchildren. Two of my grandchildren, Kevin

Christophel and Ross Lugasi, are part of a grass cutting business that was started as an offshoot from the Janosik enterprise. The business is supervised by one of my employees, Grayson Hurley, who does maintenance and landscaping for the Johnny Janosik complex. The grass cutting business became a way for my grandchildren to learn the value of hard work and the pride of making their own money. Their business is no small undertaking, as these three fellows spend every summer cutting about 50 acres of properties throughout Laurel. They cut some of the properties, like my yard, twice a week. I now have a 10-year-old granddaughter who wants to join the business next summer.

I'm proud of the hard work that these youth put in and feel good that they're learning a valuable lesson. They're learning that satisfaction is earned, not free; and it's important that, even as young people, they become a productive part of society. I'm afraid that, as parents, we sometimes allow our kids to be glued to the television screen and don't assert the influence necessary to help them, early on, become contributors to society.

I'm thankful that God allows hard work and common sense to be ingredients for success. If success depended on being extremely intelligent, I probably would have never gotten out of Hopewell, Virginia. You don't have to be the smartest person on earth—just willing to work twice as hard.

A local favorite for Laurel citizens in the early 1960s was the sidewalk sale at Johnny Janosik's Television and Appliance. Johnny and his staff would place certain televisions and appliances out on the sidewalk in front of his store, and patrons would "stake a claim" while waiting for the opportunity to purchase their item.

Chapter 6 • *Don't Forget Who Brung You to the Dance*

I've always found that associating with good people keeps you grounded and full of positive energy. I try to watch successful and positive people and learn from them. Most important, I'm not afraid to ask questions. Amazingly, many people, when faced with a problem, feel somehow embarrassed to ask for help. I say, "Ask for help! Don't sweat it."

I didn't attain a high level of book-learned education, but I do have eyes to watch, ears to hear, and a mouth to ask the right questions. God gave us all some basic abilities. I think how you apply them promotes success in life. We have to be bold sometimes and not be afraid to step out and take a chance. But common sense always takes the lead in any wise decision.

"Getting there" is hard enough. "Staying there" and keeping focused is the real challenge. Let's take a look at the kind of people who can help or hinder our progress.

It's all about relationships

Paul Broyhill, Jr., of Broyhill Industries, was on hand to help Johnny and Mary Louise Janosik with the grand opening of their new furniture store on US 13, Laurel, in 1978. Pictured are (left to right): Broyhill, Mary Louise, then-Laurel Mayor Bill Horner, and Johnny.

Chapter 7

REMAINING 'UNDER THE INFLUENCE'

*L*ooking back over the years, I've found a common denominator that exists as a major dynamic in my personal and business life successes. Whether it's the actual physical success of the furniture business today, or my personal success in surviving at the age of 16 when I first came to Laurel, Delaware, good people were in the mix.

God has graced me with a tendency to connect myself with good, positive, success-oriented people. I've always found myself to be somewhat of a lone wolf. I try to isolate myself from the fads and trends that society throws at us. Growing up, I can vividly recall many of my classmates at Hopewell High School developing various social cliques and spending ungodly hours hanging out on a street corner or wasting time in some other way.

Nothing has changed. Today, young people still "hang out." I'm certainly not implying that anything is wrong with that. But I could never fit into that type of mold. In my opinion, time spent standing around gets in the way of getting things done.

I've always tried to distance myself from people who hang out and sleep in. Far too much needs to be done for anyone to allow himself or herself to fall into a routine of non-activity. I know it's extremely important that people stay focused, develop a plan, and work the plan. Inactivity in itself is a distraction. Distractions cause us to lose our focus and purpose in life.

I suppose by today's medical standards I would have been diagnosed with classic Attention Deficit Disorder. If not for my sheer determination to teach myself to stay focused, I would only spend a limited amount of time on any given activity before feeling the need to start another project. I think the fact that I work diligently to complete one job before engaging in another helps to keep a healthy balance.

So I've never been a person who does a lot of hanging out, whether on a street corner or in a local bar. Maybe I have a natural, built-in mechanism that helps me avoid the kinds of people who drain my energy through inactivity. Instead, I've found myself surrounded by people who have a similar desire for staying active and focused.

Even though a good many of the people who have been "energizers" in my life have passed on, I still find myself inspired by my recollections of them. We all have certain people who touch our lives and cause us to see a direct connection between our association with them and the successes we enjoy today.

At 77 years of age, I've decided to make a concerted effort to sit down and recall the fine people and the positive impact they've had on my life.

I must include my mother and father on my list of positive influences. Hold on a minute. Maybe you're thinking, "Why on earth would you put them first?"

Sure, at times I reflect on my childhood and feel I was deprived of parental guidance. I may have even lacked a true sense of the maternal and paternal bond that is very important to a young child. (Perhaps that's why my relationship with my wife and children plays such a vital role in my life.) No, I didn't have the perfect parents—far from it. I wasn't abused—well, perhaps neglected at times—but I survived. In all fairness, I believe my parents truly did the best they knew how.

Mom lacked any formal education and was unable to accept the sacrificial commitment that goes with being a wife and raising children in an environment of adversity. Dad totally immersed himself in work, trying to make a living, and somehow lost sight of his family and its need for his guidance. Mom and Dad did not intentionally abandon us emotionally; the problem was simply an issue of hard times, both inside and outside the Janosik household.

Then there was Aunt Katy. She and Uncle Joe lived not too far from where I grew up. The thing I remember most about Aunt Katy is her cooking. I recall that I would get hungry and go to Aunt Katy's house and literally hang around there until she would have to feed me just to get rid of me.

I consider discipline extraordinarily important in any person's life. A lack of discipline creates a lack of focus and commitment. Whenever I think of discipline, a certain face comes to mind. It's the face of Sister Mary Elaine who made a significant contribution to my young life while I attended St. James Parochial School in Hopewell. She had a no-nonsense educational philosophy and would not tolerate rude behavior. Almost single-handedly, she made me aware that any insubordinate action would have an equally undesirable reaction. In no way do I support or condone physical abuse. I'm afraid, however, that in many ways we've made our current educators powerless to maintain order in the classroom. Teachers and school administrators are not respected, and fear of lawsuits keeps them from creating the kind of disciplined environment that Sister Mary Elaine provided for me.

My list would certainly not be complete without including Mary Goff and her son, Jack.

This mother and son were the reason I came to live in Laurel, Delaware. Jack was my best friend and somebody I could always depend on when I needed a hand. Not only was Mary Goff responsible for seeing that I had somewhere to live when I came to Laurel back in 1942, but she was also my mother's dearest friend and a friend to my family while I was growing up in Hopewell. Few people have the spirit and resolve of Mary Goff. At 95 years of age, Mary is an ongoing inspiration and positive influence in my life. This world would be a lot more enjoyable with a few more Mary Goffs.

During a visit to his native community of Hopewell, Virginia, Johnny stopped to see the home of his Aunt Katy and Uncle Joe. It was here that he was able to get many home-cooked meals as a young boy.

Also, Bob Brody and his mother, Mary, helped keep me fed in those lean years. Bob and I played ball together in the old Sharptown Baseball League. After the games, I would go to his house for his mom's home-cooked meals. I think I developed a knack for finding places to get a meal.

Several people come to mind when I consider the support and encouragement that came at a time when my life was filled with fear and uncertainty. At the age of 16, having just arrived in Laurel with two dollars and a clothing bag, I literally had no idea what I should do next. But I knew I wanted to get my high school diploma, a commodity that was scarce in my immediate family. Though the value of education and obtaining my diploma was important to me, I couldn't escape the fact that I was on my own and barely making enough money to survive. It wouldn't have taken much for me to simply give up the idea of school and pour myself into a job that paid 50 cents an hour. Several dedicated individuals understood my plight and took the time to encourage me.

George Schollenberger, the Laurel High School football coach and a local icon, was one of them. Coach Schollenberger was an intimidating

Johnny (left) and friend Bob Brody, spent a lot of time together as they were growing up. Both played baseball for the "Sharptown Eagles," which was part of the Eastern Shore Baseball League. They also played softball for a team sponsored by Johnny's employer, Osbourne Hudson.

Chapter 7 • Remaining 'Under the Influence'

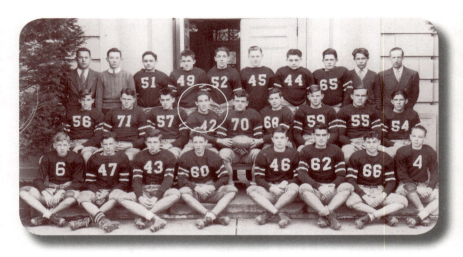

Johnny Janosik (#42) was active on the Laurel High School football team during the 1942-43 season. He played under local high school sports legend, Coach George Schollenberger (pictured far left, top row). Also pictured (far right) is Laurel High School Athletic Director, T. Robert Ruston.

man who could be pretty tough on his players. But he knew my situation and how tempted I was to quit school for full-time employment. Coach Schollenberger was impressed with my speed and agility and offered me a first-string spot on the football squad. I remember meeting with him in his office to discuss it.

I must have been a comical sight. At 5 feet 6 inches tall, I weighed in at 121 pounds and had stuffed a pack of Lucky Strike cigarettes in my pocket. I guess I thought the cigarettes made me appear more mature and tougher than I felt. Up to that point I was somewhat of a stranger in Laurel and wondered if I would ever fit in. After all, there weren't many Slovak-Catholics in rural Sussex County, Delaware. I was excited about the offer to join the team but a bit shocked when Coach Schollenberger yanked the cigarettes out of my pocket and announced, "You won't be needing these anymore."

He was right. I never smoked again. I went on to play for the 1942-43 Laurel High School football team and wound up playing not only football but basketball and baseball, as well. I lettered in all three sports.

It wasn't all glory, though. Looking back, I must have been a bigger challenge to Coach Schollenberger than I realized. A particular fall day in 1942 will go down in history as one of the worst days of my life. It was just after the annual Seaford-Laurel football game, a sporting event that had become a tradition as the two rival schools faced off on the field every Thanksgiving Day.

Johnny (#27) was passionate about sports as a young man. Here he is with the 1942-43 Laurel High School basketball team.

Chapter 7 • Remaining 'Under the Influence'

Just after the Thanksgiving holidays, our football team had our yearbook photos taken on the steps of the high school. Our group photo captured us wearing uniforms that had just been cleaned.

As soon as the photographer let us go, someone noticed that the football field behind the school was extremely muddy from a recent heavy rainfall. This presented an extraordinary temptation to us. Teachers were in school, which left the team with a false sense of security as we set off to play an unscheduled, and completely illegal, scrimmage game on the muddy field. After playing, we all went in, changed our clothes and left our muddy uniforms stacked in the school gymnasium.

As if this was not enough of a youthful demonstration of rebellion, a number of us decided we would take some (or all) of the school day off, unexcused. It was our first-string football team members who made this very unwise decision. As I remember it, teammate Lester Downes and I took off four hours from school; Bill Purnell took six hours; and Hilton Messick took the entire day off. Bob Henry, who had a broken ankle, left school for only two hours.

But, as we all know, for every action there is a reaction. Little did we know that as we enjoyed a short vacation from school, our future was about to be uncomfortably affected. When we returned to school, our football team was greeted by the wrath of school principal, Mr. Dickerson, and coach Schollenberger.

There was no guesswork involved in identifying the guilty players as they had the dirty football uniforms bearing their team numbers stacked in the gymnasium. Principal Dickerson decided that our childish prank, especially the fact that we skipped school, would be met with a severe punishment.

He ordered the members of our first string squad who had skipped school to line up in the hallway. He then brought out a large, wooden paddle that was shaped like a tennis racquet. The paddle had a number of three-quarter-inch holes drilled in it. He told us that we would receive "two licks" for each hour we had taken off from school unexcused. I am sure the looks on our faces showed that we were horrified.

One by one, we were made to bend over as Principal Dickerson applied the paddle. I remember being so ashamed that I had to endure this for skipping school.

I'm sure there are those who would consider the punishment my teammates and I received as abuse. I disagree. We deserved the punishment we got. We knew what we did was wrong, but that did not stop us. One thing is for sure, I never skipped school again! And to the best of my knowledge, neither did any of the others who were involved in this incident. In my opinion, the punishment fit the crime, and it accomplished the goal of teaching us a major lesson in responsibility and accountability. That is what discipline is all about. It really straightened us out.

Many people looked after me, took special care to meet with me, and helped me do what was necessary to remain in school. They were biology teacher T. Allen Phillips, Laurel High School principal Chester Dickerson, and school superintendent Charlie P. Helm. Mr. Helm even offered to have me move into his home because he knew I was living in a boarding house by myself. As generous as his offer was, I didn't see it as a sensible option—mainly because I didn't like how living with the school superintendent would appear to the other kids at school. Mr. Dickerson also helped me get into his bookkeeping class. I had no idea then how important that class would be in my future. And T. Allen Phillips—what would I have done without him? He took me under his wing as a mentor and was constantly boosting my morale. These three men had more faith in me than I did in myself.

After I graduated from high school, Franklin Oliphant helped me get into the workforce. Franklin's father, C.C. Oliphant, started a sheet metal and roofing business a number of years earlier. After his father died, Franklin took over the family business and hired me. I not only worked at C.C. Oliphant doing sheet metal work but also became good friends with Franklin. He owned a 35-foot pleasure boat, docked at Indian River on the east side of Sussex County. I think I appreciated Franklin's spirit for adventure and his keen business sense as much as I appreciated the money I was making at his metal fabrication company. I see Franklin as a major influence on my life as it pertains to my own business philosophy.

Another influential person in my life was Nan Fooks Campbell. In 1960, she arranged for me to rent a store in one of her downtown buildings. I think Miss Nan took a liking to me and wanted to help me get better established. I was expanding our television repair business and really had no experience in purchasing property; but in 1961 Miss Nan came to me and suggested I buy the building where I worked. It had 18 units with offices and apartments, and I saw right away it could provide a great financial resource through commercial and residential rentals. The building was worth every bit of $60,000. To my amazement, when Miss Nan approached me, she offered the building to me for $25,000. I went to Farmer's Bank across the street and, within a day or two, I'd made my first major purchase. Over the past 40 years, I've made quite a few major purchases, but Miss Nan got me started and helped to build my confidence. Miss Nan died a few years later of cancer, and in the 1980s I sold the building that used to be hers for about $185,000.

I cannot forget the people who made up the Board of Directors of the Laurel Farmer's Bank, including Franklin Oliphant. As businessmen, they took little time to recognize not only the value of the Nan Fooks Campbell building but also my own potential as a hardworking businessman (though I was far from seasoned at the time). The board included Laurel Flour Mill owner Elwood Chipman, who today has a pond named in his honor; Laurence Allen, an area property owner; and Howard Elliott, bank president. They all made me feel that I could be trusted and said they saw that I had the makings of a good businessman.

Though he represented a different bank, I must be quick to acknowledge the support I received from Sussex Trust Bank manager Harold Smith. It was 1953, and I needed money to go into my own business. I had come back from military service at the close of World War II and recently left my television repair technician job with RCA in Easton, Maryland.

Once again, I was back in Laurel without a penny in my pocket. I shared my business plan with Harold.

While I had no money and no collateral, I had a vision, and he must have sensed my passion. With nothing more than the signatures of Mary Louise and me, Harold Smith loaned $900 to the business. I bought an old Jeep station wagon, and it became my service truck. Within 90 days, I was able to pay off the $900 loan, and I've been in business ever since.

Sound advice has always been worth more to me than anything money can buy. Much can be learned from people who have experience. Such is the case with two other fine Laurel businessmen.

One is former Delaware Governor Elbert Carvel. Governor Carvel led the state for two administrations. His family fertilizer business brought him from upstate New York to Laurel. He maintained an office in the Valiant Fertilizer building, just a few blocks from our store. Every morning the Governor would walk by our store on the way to his office. There were few times he did not stop and chat with me on his way to work. I recall those as some of the most enlightening and encouraging talks of my life. The Governor has always been full of wisdom and has a knack for sharing just the right information to fit the day. Now in his mid-90s, Governor Carvel still resides in Laurel and possesses all the charm and wisdom that helped win him the governorship.

The other significant person and a man of great wisdom was Frank Calio, Sr. I think I held Mr. Calio in special esteem because, like my family, he was an immigrant. He had an appreciation for the opportunities available in the United States, and he took advantage of them. A shoemaker and repairman, Mr. Calio operated his shop in a building just down the street from our furniture and appliance store. I would stop by there many times and share

Johnny credits many people for their influence during the development of his business in Laurel. One of those influences is former Delaware Governor Elbert Carvel. He and Johnny later became partners in helping to support a campaign to expand the Laurel Public Library.

conversation with this wise Italian man. A piece of advice I will always remember was when Mr. Calio urged me to "always keep your wheels round." He said if you don't keep your wheels round your cart will go "floppity, floppity." That meant I should always do the right thing and avoid involving myself in things that are not productive. He put it in a very interesting way, but he was absolutely right.

Today I'm very good friends with Mr. Calio's son, Frank Jr., who must have heeded his father's advice. He has served on the Laurel Town Council, was the Sussex County Economic Development Administrator, and is currently chairman of the Delaware Election Commission. All of us can look back and identify the special people in our lives—the ones who have demonstrated compassion and encouragement. It's not only important to remember these people and appreciate their contribution to our lives, but it's also necessary. Who are the people who have played the role of mentor or encourager in your life?

An even more significant consideration than the recollection of our own heroes might be to ask ourselves about our own willingness to become a special person in someone else's life. That, I believe, is our tuition in life: to help as we have been helped.

Sometimes our relationships are so wrapped up in one another, it's hard to tell who's helping whom. A number of people in my life fall into that category, and I'm eager for you to get to know them.

Leading by Example

Johnny Janosik and world famous child neurosurgeon, Dr. Ben Carson.

Chapter 8

THEY KEEP ME ON TRACK

*D*angerous. That's what it would be to try to list the names of the people who have played a vital role in my life. So many people have touched my heart I cannot possibly name them all. But if I'm to give a true account of my life and recognize pivotal times, places, and people, I must at least attempt to share the names of those who will forever have a special place in my heart—the ones who keep me on track.

I cannot help but start with the four people who know me best—my wife Mary Louise, and our daughters Linda, Tina, and Lori. My family always provides inspiration for me and certainly delivers the solace that can make even the toughest days tolerable. Mary Louise and I have taken great joy in seeing our family grow over the years. I now have a full complement of grandchildren; and, as much as I like to think I can teach these young children some valuable lessons, I find myself learning from them daily.

The thing that strikes me as most impressive about Mary Louise is her desire to think things out before making decisions. She is a mild-tempered lady, careful not to make spontaneous comments that are driven by emotion. She knows that when tempers flare or when situations call for decisions of a significant magnitude, time is a friend. While it's my nature to be quick to reply and I usually become frustrated if I can't come to a conclusion within a few moments, Mary Louise likes to think over an issue for 24 hours before responding. More often than not, after 24 hours things have a way of seeming less urgent and a bit more in perspective. Mary Louise is truly a gift from God and a blessing for our family. She has earned, and most certainly deserves, my unwavering respect.

Our daughters have all forged their lives with a sense of independence and individuality. I cannot say for sure that any of them can be compared to the others. Each has her own unique personality and formula for success.

Linda Kaye Christophel, the oldest, is nothing short of a computer wizard. She gave our business its first exposure to this modern, necessary technology and helped install the first computer network at Johnny Janosik's. Years ago, she decided that being an active member of the family business wasn't the career choice she desired, so she left the business but still maintains an interest in it. Linda Kaye and her daughters Casey and Kariane and son Kevin reside near Bethel, Delaware.

Our second oldest daughter, Christina (Tina) Marie Palmer, like her sister, decided to pursue her own career goals outside the family business. Tina is a true visionary, so I wasn't surprised when she wanted to spread her wings and move into her chosen field as a real estate agent and broker in Arnold, Maryland. Her daughter Amy is also a real estate agent, and the two work out of the same office. Tina and her husband Walter, an architect, serve as partners in area housing and commercial development. They also own and operate Arnold Farms Garden Center. Tina and Walter have another daughter, Alexandria, who is six years old.

Our youngest daughter, Lori Ann Janosik-Morrison, plays a major role in the Johnny Janosik business. Of our three girls, I think Lori Ann is the one who is most like me. I guess others who know us feel the same way because they call her "Little Johnny." Lori is a real motivator and becomes enthusiastic about any project she is involved with. At the business, Lori handles the daily monitoring of all inventory and also heads up our Charity Department. This is an area that I am most proud of because it enables the business to contribute furnishings to people who are referred by the local goodwill organization, the Good Samaritan. Working the charity end of the business is a perfect fit for Lori because she enjoys volunteering

The Janosik Family. Pictured are (left to right): Linda Kaye Christophel, Johnny, Christina (Tina) Janosik Palmer, Mary Louise, and Lori Janosik Morrison.

and organizing charity fund-raisers in the Laurel community, including her work with the local Epworth Christian School. She and her husband, Barrett, a chiropractor, reside nearby and have four children—Ross, Sally, Lindsay, and Kyle.

Outside of my faith in the Lord, my family is my foundation, the thing that keeps me grounded. The Lord expects us to take care of our families because He knows that our families are the ones who will take care of us.

Understandably, I look at my employees at Johnny Janosik as an extension of my biological family. The same components that make a family strong also make a business strong. The need for trust, understanding, compassion, and unity all come into play both at home and in the workplace. I will never be able to overstate how much I appreciate the employees who work so hard for the business.

Some, like Beverly Hastings, have been with the business for many years. Beverly started with Johnny Janosik as a bookkeeper when it opened on Market Street in downtown Laurel. For the past 35 years, Beverly has become so familiar with Johnny Janosik that she literally knows most aspects of the business. She knows the business so well that staff from every department will run to Beverly whenever they have a question.

Debbie Gaskins Quillen was fresh out of college when she came to work at the store in furniture sales. Now she heads up our Sales Training Department. Like Beverly, Debbie knows the entire makeup of the Johnny Janosik operation. Debbie gives each of our new sales staff a six-week training course in proper sales and service and makes sure they are familiar with all components of the business. When the course is over, the employees literally know where every piece of merchandise is and how each department works in the overall operation. We have quality, professional, and knowledgeable employees because of Debbie's commitment to the operation.

I have always appreciated people who pay close attention to detail. It's easy to move quickly and not pay attention to small items that can make a major difference in an operation like Johnny Janosik. Jo Ann Esham is the kind of employee who pays attention to those details. She handles our in-house accounting and is able to keep track of the financial picture in every department. Her knowledge of technology has enabled the business to implement a computer network that is fed inventory, service, and sales data via a barcode system. Using this, Jo Ann is able to provide management with daily, weekly, and monthly itemized listings of every transaction company-wide.

Jo Ann works closely with our company CPA, Tom Trice. Tom has been a wonderful resource for Johnny Janosik. His knowledge of proper financial procedure has kept us in a truly successful financial planning mode. He is astute at tracking trends in the economy and industry and has been a major force in guiding the business to the success it enjoys today.

I am constantly amazed at how committed the Johnny Janosik employees can be. I consider sales manager Betty Townsend, and our Dover, Delaware, store manager Karen Christophel as two ladies who give more than expected of them, and it shows. Their enthusiasm is contagious, and I am very fortunate to have them affiliated with the business.

The same is true with warehouse manager Norman Narcisa. He worked at the Dover store as a maintenance man where he caught the eye of Karen Christophel. She knew the Laurel store was looking for someone to head up the warehouse operation and felt confident Norman was the man for the job. She was right.

Norman retired from the United States Air Force where he was stationed at the nearby Dover Air Force Base. While in the military, Norman was a load master; he supervised a large group of personnel whose job was to load the huge C-5 supply and troop planes that fly out of the Air Force base daily. His organizational skills have proven to be a major resource for the furniture operation.

Along with taking care of our warehouse, Norman oversees the maintenance of the Johnny Janosik vehicle fleet. This includes vehicles making daily deliveries and special emergency runs as well as a fleet of service trucks that do home service calls for furniture and upholstery repair. The fleet of Johnny Janosik trucks undergoes daily inspections before they are permitted to hit the road. Each driver must complete a Department of Transportation safety checklist before leaving the truck bay. An in-house vehicle service department, equipped with a full garage and maintenance crew, takes care of any problems having to do with the operation of these vehicles. Trucks are completely overhauled and fit with a new engine and transmission after 300,000 to 350,000 miles. No matter how complex things get in these operations, Norman is able to keep things running smoothly.

As I never get tired of saying, customer service makes or breaks a business. I want Johnny Janosik to be totally customer friendly. To accomplish this, we must have the ability to take care of the customer before, during, and after the sale. So within the Johnny Janosik operation there are several sub-operations.

One crew inspects all merchandise as it comes through the warehouse doors. They determine if any pieces need minor or major repair work. Our repair department is able to have this work done either right on the spot or have the merchandise transferred to our in-house upholstery and furniture repair shop. Dawn Haynes heads up this operation, and she exemplifies the customer service philosophy of the Johnny Janosik business.

On occasion, customers may discover a repair or upholstery problem with the furniture long after they've purchased it. In a case like that, Dawn sends someone to the home where the repair work is done to the customer's satisfaction. We believe in making a commitment to our customers to stand by the products that they purchase from Johnny Janosik, both during and after the sale. I believe that, in the long run, a business does itself a favor by making sure it stands by the customer.

We are fortunate to have the team of Sheila Callaway and Ginger Ayotte. Together, they assure that Johnny Janosik has top quality products that represent the most current trends in furniture. Sheila is our designated buyer. She keeps her finger on the pulse of furniture trends and prices, meets with the various vendors, and picks the finest merchandise for our sales floors. Once Sheila makes the buying decisions, Ginger uses technology to establish the connection between our store and the furniture factories. She computer orders the merchandise and keeps records of all production orders. Ginger makes sure that our sales people know when their customers' orders are here and ready for pickup or scheduled delivery.

Johnny Janosik employees do the job based on our customer service philosophy, starting right at the top with our general manager and CEO, Frank Gerardi. A former furniture store owner with five locations, Frank's knowledge of the furniture industry and his ability to think beyond the norm has helped take Johnny Janosik's annual sales from $18 million to $40 million in less than five years. After running his own furniture business and before coming on board with us, Frank worked with a national commercial liquidating firm. In his job with that organization, he helped businesses that were having cash flow problems and other financial issues go out of business quickly, without winding up bankrupt and destitute. It's very beneficial to have someone in management who has such a thorough knowledge of furniture sales and business savvy. Since Frank has been with us, Johnny Janosik Furniture has expanded its operation to Dover, Delaware.

I'm excited about the future of Johnny Janosik. You might think Mary Louise and I would be tempted to sit back and enjoy the benefits of the business as it continues its present momentum. That would certainly be a most comfortable and risk-free way to determine Johnny Janosik's business future. But the business is simply too important for us just to sit back and allow it to become idle or, worse, turn stagnant. To do that would be unfair to the employees, to the community, and even to the state. Great things are in store for Johnny Janosik, and these great things can provide our employee team and our customers with many benefits.

How can I say this? Well, look at what's on the drawing board. We recently purchased a 17-acre field along U. S. 13, south of Dover. Our plan is to sell our two stores in Dover and develop the farmland into one huge retail complex. In Laurel we're presently working to double our warehouse space and enhance our showroom area. Our sales reports show that we're on track to support these expansions. We're pressing on toward the goal of increasing our workforce from its present 300 employees to between 350 and 400 employees.

While vacationing in Florida, Johnny and Mary Louise stopped in North Carolina to visit a legendary figure in the furniture world, Paul Broyhill, Sr., of Broyhill Industries.

I have a real "dream team" of employees of over 300 hard-working, dedicated people who trust Johnny Janosik to help them raise and take care of their families. I am proud of the contribution each member of our team makes to the success of the business.

When I consider this smooth-running team of workers, I become inspired and excited to be the namesake of the Johnny Janosik organization. These individuals pull together to make sure that our customers are treated with the respect and courtesy they deserve. They are the reason that Mary Louise and I are so proud of creating this business called Johnny Janosik.

Oh, I like to work hard, that's for sure. But I also like to play hard and sometimes live dangerously. Come on along . . . let's take a little bumpy ride down memory lane.

"The Dream Team." Johnny considers some of the employees at his store to be his closest friends. Pictured here is the management staff of Johnny Janosik Furniture Store in Laurel, Delaware. Pictured are (left to right): Jo Ann Esham, Beverly Hastings, Sheila Callaway, Dawn Haynes, and Betty Townsend. Standing (left to right): Debbie Gaskins Quillen, Ginger Ayotte, Norman Narcissa, and Frank Gerardi.

Johnny and Mary Louise attended a 2002 holiday party with good friends Dr. Benjamin Carson of Johns Hopkins Hospital, Baltimore, and his wife Candy.

Johnny has a special place in his heart for young people. He is dedicated to helping support educational programs for at-risk and challenged youth. Pictured here, Johnny speaks to a group of young people at the Sussex County Opportunities Program in Education (SCOPE) in Bridgeville, Delaware.

During his career in Laurel, Johnny has been awarded a number of special community honors, including "Citizen of the Year." Here, Johnny poses with others who have received the honor, including former Delaware Governor Elbert Carvel.

Chapter 9

TRUTH IS
THE BEST DEFENSE

I have always heard, "If you want something done, give the job to a busy man." Being busy for the sake of being busy isn't necessarily productive; but when you enjoy being busy as well as getting things done, you have a great combination! It's always worked for me. I'm one of those people who just needs to be busy. But not everything I do is a matter of great importance to anybody but me. True, I keep the business and my charity work as a top priority, but some things I do just for fun. I'm talking about the satisfaction I've found in what I consider to be my personal hobbies. I've had several passions in life, outside of my family and the business, of course. And it's interesting to discover that there's almost always a fine line between my work and play.

One of my hobbies is home restoration. Over the years I've renovated and restored over a dozen houses and commercial properties in the Laurel area, including the 129-year-old home near Portsville where my wife and I have lived for almost 25 years. I also restored my wife's family home just outside of Laurel, near Sycamore. My granddaughter actually lives in the historic "Prettyman Home"

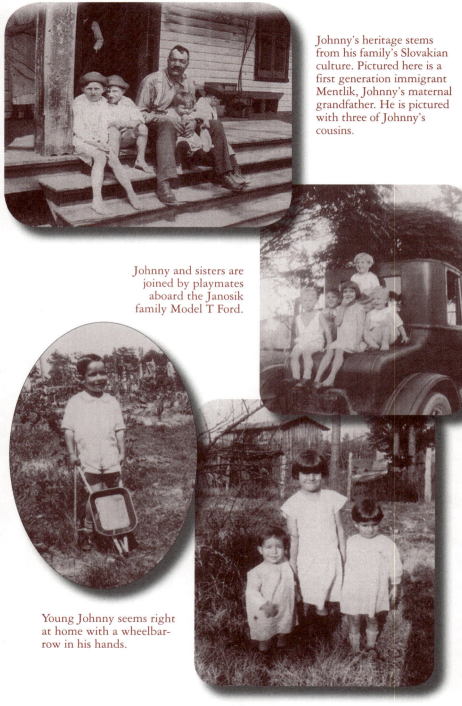

Johnny's heritage stems from his family's Slovakian culture. Pictured here is a first generation immigrant Mentlik, Johnny's maternal grandfather. He is pictured with three of Johnny's cousins.

Johnny and sisters are joined by playmates aboard the Janosik family Model T Ford.

Young Johnny seems right at home with a wheelbarrow in his hands.

A toddler, Johnny is shown with two of his cousins when he lived in Hopewell, Virginia.

While attending St. James Catholic School, Johnny was able to catch the streetcar near his Hopewell home. Today the streetcar station is a tavern.

Father, John Janosik, Sr., with three of his children: Johnny, Evelyn and Billy.

Johnny at home in Hopewell, Virginia.

A young Johnny Janosik stands in the yard of his Hopewell, Virginia, home.

Johnny's father, John Janosik, Sr.

Johnny's mother, Emily.

Johnny and sister Mary get some advice from their father, John Janosik, Sr.

Billy's naval portrait.

Johnny and his brother Billy had a very close relationship while growing up in Hopewell, Virginia.

Johnny Janosik and his Laurel High School graduating class of 1943.

The Osbourne Hudson softball team. Johnny (bottom right) is pictured here with his teammates, including good friend Bob Brody (top left).

Johnny considers the renovation, building, and development of residential housing to be a one of his favorite hobbies. Pictured here (top to bottom) are some of the projects he has been personally involved with: the 10th Street townhouse project in Laurel with 21 units; the home he and Mary Louise share near Portsville; and a civil war-era home he renovated known as "The Prettyman Home."

which I restored in downtown Laurel. That home is pre-Civil War. I guess my love for restoration really started after I bought the downtown commercial building from Miss Nan Fooks in the early 60s and restored the 18 upstairs apartment units and the street level storefronts. Just recently, I was able to build a 21-unit townhouse project in Laurel. Watching these projects come to life is very rewarding. I also have a love for cars. At one point, I owned a 1967 Ford Mustang, a 1965 Ford Thunderbird, and 1959, 1961 and 1963 Corvettes. Back in the late 1960s I found these cars in various places and was able to purchase all of them for a total of about $6,000. I fell on hard times, however, and wound up selling the whole lot for $11,000. Come to think of it, I guess that hobby turned into a pretty decent investment. And, as personal entertainment goes, it was pretty safe.

I can't say that about another hobby that I came to enjoy a great deal—flying. When I was serving in the Navy, I always thought I'd like to learn to be a carrier pilot. At the end of my service time, I was offered pilot training, but I turned it down because, after almost three years in the Pacific Ocean, I was in a hurry to get home.

A good friend of mine in Laurel, Irving Tyndall, was a pilot, and he was aware of my desire to fly. In 1947, he helped get me involved in flight training. He had a small Piper Cub of his own and took me flying quite a few times. One time, in particular, brings back a bittersweet memory.

Irving had agreed to take me back to Hopewell, Virginia, to visit my family. We flew out of Laurel and, for some reason, missed our designated landing point of Petersburg, Virginia. I don't know what happened, but back in those days, compasses ran the entire flight; we lacked the sophisticated operational equipment that is standard in small planes today. Nonetheless, we were able to land in Waverly, Virginia, where we took a small break and then made

The Model T Ford that Johnny Janosik has restored is a parade favorite in the community of Laurel.

In the mid-1980s, Johnny and friend Bob Lake, a Delaware State Trooper, had a special partnership which involved buying shrimp in Florida and having Lake fly it back to Sussex County for sale at a roadside seafood stand. Pictured here is the small Cessna 340 airplane used for the venture.

preparations to head on to Petersburg.

The Piper Cub had no automatic starting mechanism, so the propeller had to be hand cranked. I told Irving that I would crank the prop and went about getting the prop into starting position. Little did I know that Irving had the ignition on. The engine fired when I pulled down on the propeller, and it cut an eight-inch gash in my leg. The gash was so deep I could see my leg bone through the mangled flesh.

The airport operator knew a doctor in the area, so Irving rushed me over, and I got 30 to 40 stitches. Immediately after the surgery, I was back aboard the plane, heading for Hopewell. That was a Sunday, and I was back in Laurel in time for work on Monday morning. I remember I was working at Osbourne Hudson's shop doing radio repair work. I didn't miss any time because of the accident, and I tried to work without drawing too much attention to my injury—not because I was so dedicated but because the mistake was so stupid that I didn't want to have to explain it.

I spent most of the day sitting at my workbench, so few people were actually aware of my injury. When I did have to walk across the room with an obvious limp, I just told people that I had been playing football down in Hopewell and injured my leg in the mobile home park. It's still amazing to me that, after having such a major injury, I was able to move right on with the plane trip and then be back to work the next day. If this type of accident happened today, I'd be a lot more truthful about it—and more sensible, too. Most likely, I'd be looking at a three-day stay in the hospital.

As for my friend Irving Tyndall, he went on to serve as a fighter pilot during the Korean Conflict and was killed when his plane was shot down over Korea in 1950. I wish he could have been around to share my joy when I went on to get my pilot's license and eventually purchase my own small plane.

My fondness for flying and love of planes continued to grow over the years. In the mid-1980s, a friend of mine, Delaware State Trooper Bob Lake, was working to get his flight miles logged to obtain his pilot instructor's license. At the time, I was selling Black Bart wood stoves to dealers throughout the region, including Delaware, Maryland, Pennsylvania, and New Jersey. I hired Bob to take me to meetings with the dealers. It was a win-win situation. Bob was able to get his flight time logged in, and I could meet with several dealers in a record time.

Johnny spent a great deal of time with pilot friend Irving Tyndall (pictured) in the late 1940s. It was Tyndall who helped Johnny get his pilot's license. A member of the United States Air Force, Tyndall was later killed during a flight mission over Korea in 1950.

Bob had flown down to Florida on occasion and found that shrimp were plentiful and inexpensive. He talked to me about joining him in buying shrimp, flying it back to Delaware, and selling it for a significant profit. This idea seemed great to me. So, in short order, we went into the freelance shrimp business.

The shrimp business became profitable to the point that we were selling everything Bob could haul up from Florida. He had his retail shrimp stand at Massey's Landing, near Pot-Nets Communities. Bob stripped all the seats out of the plane and made more room to haul shrimp. He was flying down to Florida twice a week, and the shrimp sold just about as fast as we could unload them in Delaware. Everything was working out really well because, again, Bob was getting his flight time, I was enjoying the flying, and shrimp sales were booming.

And then I made a bad decision. I thought I might like to run for an open seat on the Sussex County Council. It amazes me that something as basic to our freedom here in the United States as running for public office can turn out to be such an extremely trying ordeal.

In the early 1960s, Johnny moved his television repair service out of his home and into a storefront in Laurel's downtown. The business grew to include television repair service and television and appliance sales. Johnny poses in front of the store.

I had support for the Sussex Council candidacy, but I also had my detractors. Unfortunately, it seems in many cases, those who oppose you carry the loudest voice. In the midst of my Council campaign, someone started a rumor that I was flying drugs in from Florida. The shrimp business Bob Lake and I had been operating suddenly became the foundation for this ludicrous rumor. If it were not so tragic, I could almost sit back and laugh. The idea to buy and sell the shrimp was a good one, and it was successful. It's also an example of simple, well-planned entrepreneurship.

Thanks to some troublemakers and their obvious disdain for me, rumors of drug sales were being offered as an explanation for why I was a successful businessman. This ridiculous rumor has little or no detrimental effect on me today, but I cannot help but be hurt by the fact that anyone would insinuate that the Johnny Janosik business success is based on anything except hard work and determination. To me, that idea is unfair to my family and to the scores of employees who have worked so hard to make the business into the shining example it is today.

> *" I have done nothing that others could not have done as long as they were willing to work hard and live clean. "*

I have no desire to blow my own horn. The evidence of my life's work and personal interests speak for themselves. The important thing to remember is that I have done nothing that others could not have done as long as they were willing to work hard and live clean.

That is the core of what I believe is so great about living in the United States. The fact that a skinny, poor Slovak boy could step

Chapter 9 • *Truth is the Best Defense*

off a bus with less than two dollars in his pocket, work to develop a major business that contributes significantly to the state's economy and to the local quality of life—and have a little fun along the way—is nothing short of miraculous. I'm proud to say that the respect that has come to the Johnny Janosik business has been nothing short of earned.

You know, you can have everything in the world going for you—loving spouse, thriving business, exciting activities—but without your health it doesn't amount to a pile of peanuts. I ought to know.

Chapter 10

MORE LIVES THAN A CAT

A friend once told me that I have as many lives as a cat. I suppose considering the times I have been bruised and beaten in traffic crashes and work related fiascoes, she was not far from being correct. I've been blessed with great resiliency and the ability to get up whenever something or somebody is trying to hold me down.

I'm keenly aware of the need to develop a proactive attitude as it pertains to health issues. I maintain a health regimen that includes regularly scheduled checkups with the doctor and on-going rehabilitative sessions. I stay extremely active and think this goes a long way in helping to keep my body's defenses strong.

I know that, well into my 70s, I need to be careful and take special precautions—especially since I have a tendency to fall victim to illnesses and am accident prone.

In the summer of 1997, my wife and I had started jogging each morning as a means of exercise. We would go with friends, and because we live in a rural area, the running was actually relaxing and enjoyable with the natural scenery.

One morning, I found myself lagging behind the others. I began to taste the saliva filling my mouth and suddenly felt as though a bear were hugging me around the chest. I remember so well joking with my wife and the others about the prospects of it being a heart attack.

Mary Louise called Dr. Vance Prewitt, our family physician, and he immediately did an EKG which indicated abnormalities in my heart activity. The EKG showed that I was experiencing something known as "ischemia." Ischemic heart disease is the technical term for obstruction of blood flow to the heart. I learned that this is the result of excess fat or plaque deposits narrowing the veins that supply oxygenated blood to the heart. At age 72, I had developed coronary artery disease.

Dr. Prewitt ordered a heart catheterization, a medical procedure in which a thin tube called a catheter is inserted into a small puncture in the groin, arm, or wrist, and then fed through a blood vessel to the heart. The physician is able to track the course of the catheter by watching it on a fluoroscope, which displays the blood vessels on a monitor screen. By using this procedure, the doctors were able to locate where the blockages were and how badly they were affecting my heart.

With six arteries at least 99 percent blocked up with the deposits, they scheduled me for heart bypass surgery right away. Doctors at Peninsula Regional Medical Center in Salisbury, Maryland, were able to graft all six blockages with five artery bypasses. I thought surely I'd be laid up after the surgery for at least six to nine months. The fact is, within 30 days I was driving again. I'm not saying this schedule is the correct one, or even safe recovery, but it worked for me.

I'm determined not to lie around and let illness take control. If at all possible, I will never let an illness take hold of me without a fight. I made sure that, however active the doctors and nurses wanted me to be following the surgery, I did twice as much. I continue to have regular checkups for my heart; so far, in the five years since my surgery, I've remained free of the deadly blockages. But I'm smart enough to know that once you've shown the symptoms of coronary artery disease you must work to maintain a healthy diet and an active lifestyle. I count myself lucky that I had symptoms to warn me of the problems of my heart.

For some unfortunate people, the first symptom is a massive heart attack that becomes their last symptom, as well. According to medical experts, almost one million Americans die of cardiovascular disease each year—42 percent of all deaths. It's the leading cause of death for Americans ages 35 and older. I think, like me, most people believe that heart disease is something that hits only the elderly. Actually, of the one million people who die each year of heart disease, 160,000 are between 35 and 64 years of age. I hope that people who may be at risk for heart disease will not wait until they have symptoms before being checked by their doctors. This is actually a disease that can be kept in check with proper medicine, diet and exercise.

I will always tout the importance of being proactive when it comes to dealing with illnesses. For instance, every man over 50 years of age should have a prostate examination annually. Like heart disease, I learned firsthand the importance of proactive medical checkups.

At the age of 65, I was encouraged by Dr. Prewitt to have a prostate specific antigen (PSA) screening. A PSA test tells the doctor the level of prostate specific antigen in the blood, just as a cholesterol test can tell a doctor the levels of cholesterol in the blood. Health experts say the average, healthy 50-year-old male should have a PSA of less than 4.0 nanograms per milliliter of blood (4.0 ng/ml). My PSA read 6.9 ng/ml, which Dr. Prewitt confirmed was "high."

Trouble? Yes. I had a tumor in my prostate. My choices were to have treatments to try to dissolve the tumor or to move ahead with surgery. All I could think about was the fact that I still had plenty of things I wanted to do. So I instructed doctors to go ahead with the surgery.

The tumor was removed and now, 12 years later, I have no recurring problems. I was only in the hospital for about four days. I guess I have a high tolerance for pain, so I worked hard to keep moving and not allow myself to stiffen up immediately following the surgery. I just believed that I did not need to add misery to misery, so I pushed myself to be active. I think this attitude helped my recovery immeasurably.

A couple of years following the prostate surgery, I developed a hernia. Some people think there may be a relationship between the prostate surgery and an eventual hernia. The only thing that

I know for sure is that most of the people I talked to who had prostate cancer surgery reported that they also followed up a year or two later with a hernia. So this is not a scientific study, but it does give cause for thought.

The hernia operation was not something I looked forward to but as anyone who has had a hernia can attest, not having the surgery was an equally dismal consideration. I know that today's medical procedures allow hernia operations to be done using laparoscopic techniques. These involve small cuts in the groin area with the surgery being done inside the body while the doctors watch on a television screen. This technique makes for a much quicker recovery. Could I take advantage of the new technique? Nope. I had to have the old fashioned surgery where recovery is longer and more painful. Once again, the key to my recovery came with a willingness to move about, even when moving was a painstaking endeavor. The more I made myself get out of bed and become active, the closer I got to full recovery.

Let me be sure you understand. I'm no fan of surgical procedures, but they are a necessary evil. Most important, if the time should arise when we're faced with the need for such measures, we shouldn't put it off.

Such is the case with the surgeries I've had to undergo for back problems. In the early 1990s I slipped while carrying a case of soft drinks. Eventually, I was diagnosed with bone spurs in L-4 and L-5 vertebrae, which were compressing the spinal cord. The pain became so excruciating that I had to get something done to help deal with it.

Doctors scheduled several tests and procedures and, in due time, I was slated for a procedure called a "milogram" to determine where the problem originated. In this medical procedure the doctor injects a dye into the spinal area. I was instructed to lie very still during and after the procedure. Knowing my addiction to activity, do you think this might have been difficult for me? Yes. But I was pretty well motivated to comply as they explained that failure to follow this order could result in paralysis. The doctors were able to see the problem and perform surgery to remove the bone spurs, and I managed to keep very still.

Ten years later, I was faced with a resurrection of the back pain. Several tests were conducted, including another milogram. This time, however, the procedure had advanced so much that it was performed and I was hardly even aware it had occurred. I was diagnosed and found to need surgery to fuse the L4 and L5 vertebrae. The prognosis was not good. Doctors said within five years I would be in a wheelchair. No way could I allow that to happen! Surgery was performed, and special plates were inserted to keep pressure off the spine. Today, I feel strong and healthy with no complaints of back problems.

The important thing I stress to friends who are facing surgery or other medical procedures is to move quickly. Don't put off something that has been identified as the course of action to deal with a serious medical problem. I know people who fear the unknown so much that they hold off medical efforts that could very well save their lives.

At my age, it seems more important than ever to monitor my health. I appreciate the work that hospitals and doctors do, but I don't enjoy being under their care for any length of time. It's unfortunate that I've had to be in and out of the hospital so many times in my life, but I think it helps me appreciate the work the medical professionals do.

I've also been around long enough to have old injuries and ailments come back to irritate me. Two of my recent stays in the hospital were directly linked to medical problems from over 40 years ago.

One morning, while taking a shower, I began to feel dizzy and thought I might pass out. Not wanting to fall on the hard surface of the bathtub or the wooden floor, I got out of the shower and made my way to the carpeted floor just outside the bathroom door. Resting my back against the wall, I allowed myself to slip down the surface of the wall and sit on the floor. I realized that if I passed out, my wife wouldn't hear me and may not even be aware I was having a problem. Inching my body down the stairs to the living room, I managed to get Mary's attention and let her know I needed to get to the hospital.

I was taken to Peninsula Regional Medical Center in Salisbury, Maryland, where I was admitted in early October 2002. My doctors discovered a bleeding ulcer and said I had lost about three pints of blood. No wonder I was so weak!

And guess what? The doctors also said the bleeding ulcer was located in the same spot I'd previously had ulcers back in 1958. Apparently the medication I was taking to relieve some of the pain from my shoulder joint problem had caused erosion that revived the bleeding ulcer. They gave me two units of blood and took me off the pain medicine. After several days, I regained my strength and left the hospital—but not for long.

Unable to take anything for the pain, the misery I'd been experiencing in my right shoulder increased. Doctors diagnosed this problem as a deterioration of my shoulder, stemming from the 1958 accident where my car collided with a tractor-trailer. I was told that the padding between the bones in my shoulder (known as the "Bursar Bag") had deteriorated, and I was now dealing with a bone-on-bone rubbing that was destroying my shoulder. Doctors said that oftentimes people my age decide against surgery; however, the pain was excruciating, so I gave doctors the go-ahead for a shoulder replacement operation.

In mid-December 2002, just two months after my treatment for bleeding ulcers, I was admitted back into the hospital where I underwent the shoulder replacement. I was very satisfied with the procedure and found the surgery to be nowhere near as bad as I'd expected.

Recovery, on the other hand, is another issue. The medical professionals who give physical therapy take a great deal of pride in their work and do everything they can to help their patients regain full mobility, if possible. I'm amazed at the range of motion I now have. In only three weeks I had twice the range of motion in my right arm that I had previously been experiencing years before the surgery. It is very painful to have to endure the shoulder therapy, but it has been extremely successful, and I deeply appreciate the hard work and dedication of the health professionals at PRMC.

I look back on my life and recognize that I had the opportunity at one or more points simply to retire and allow my aches and pains to govern my life. As a matter of fact, at one time my wife and I did consider retirement. We bought a winter home in Lady Lakes, Florida, and made arrangements to turn the business over to our children.

We owned the Florida home for three years; however, in all that time, we only spent a total of 27 days there. We just couldn't let go of everything back in Laurel. I was also far from content with our lifestyle during our getaways to Florida. It seemed to be a ritual of watching television, playing golf, and eating. I realized fast that I couldn't exist in that kind of environment. The problem with retirement was easy enough to identify. I couldn't stand being around so many old people. I say that jokingly, but I really found myself wanting to get away from people who were content to just lie around and let life pass them by. I needed to be around younger, more active people. So we sold our Florida home and moved back to Laurel and resumed our place in the business.

I've come to the conclusion that there will never be life after retirement. So, as far as I am concerned, there will be no retirement. Instead, every day is a gift to be lived to its fullest, an adventure to be discovered and savored. Whether you're just starting out in life or are in your twilight years, I hope you'll agree with me that every day is invaluable, and we owe it to ourselves to make it count. Go ahead, lend a hand to someone in need. Say something encouraging. Do an unexpected favor. Practice the lost art of listening. Make a memory with a child. Don't be afraid to let your heart soar with joy or break with grief.

Even our negative experiences have value. Let me show you what I mean.

"*Go ahead!*"

Lend a hand to someone in need.
Say something encouraging.
Do an unexpected favor.
Practice the lost art of listening.
Make a memory with a child.

Chapter 11

LOOKING BACK TO FIND THE FUTURE

*T*ruly successful people never forget where they've come from. That's why I want to remember as vividly as possible what my life was like before I came to Laurel, Delaware.

The thing I remember most about my childhood was that I was always hot, cold, or hungry. True, we were poor, and we had to work hard just to survive, but not everything was bleak and cloudy. Regardless of how cold the tar paper shack we called home became or how bare the table, I was oblivious to the fact that my family was poor. It was life, the only life I knew.

Home was a three-room tar paper shack with a flat roof and no plumbing or electricity. The walls were so thin that you could punch a hole through them with your finger. In the winter, the wind would rush through every crack in the house. We had two bedrooms and a kitchen. A 36-inch high, round kerosene heater provided our heat. When Dad could afford it, we purchased a 25- or 50-pound block of ice to serve as our refrigerator. A hand pump in the kitchen provided our water supply, and outside in the neighborhood well-worn footpaths were as close as we got to roads. I recently went back to Hopewell, Virginia, and found it next to impossible to find the actual spot where our family home once stood.

The small, simple shack that was our home lacked any sense of sophistication; however, it was the place where my life's foundation was formed. When I think about that house, my parents come to mind. Even with the obvious imperfections they possessed, I found that each held certain attributes that have stayed with me, becoming a part of my makeup even today.

Dad was a workaholic and lacked the ability to show affection toward his wife and children. He often kept us at arm's length. My pattern of parenting was much the same when my girls were growing up, but now that I'm a grandfather, I've made some corrections and am more warm and approachable. On the other hand, Dad also possessed a strong determination to do what was right and provide for his family. I certainly respect that determination and consider it a valuable trait for any family man or woman.

Mom lacked the book knowledge and much of the wisdom that comes from being exposed to a structured education. She was somewhat lost regarding the simplest of parental and household duties without guidance from Dad, or even from me when Dad went away to work in Brazil. But it was her sincere innocence and pure heart that made me aware that her intentions were noble. In her own simple way, she tried to take care of us all.

That attitude is what life is all about. Nobody is really prepared for all that life dishes out. Our willingness to make at least an honest attempt to conquer the problems that come our way, however, will determine our potential for success.

A certain degree of my own success comes from the fact that, even though my parents may not have hung in there for each other, they somehow managed to give us children a fighting chance.

It breaks my heart to recall Mom's packing up my two sisters and moving out of town. I found it hard to conceal my feelings of betrayal as Mom started a second life, totally without my younger brother Billy and me. Mom remarried a number of years later to a man named Simon Moore.

As bad as life was, it would only get worse. A while after Mom left us, Dad started seeing a married woman and, in time, moved in with her. She became pregnant, but no one would admit that this was my father's child. In the meantime, the woman's husband was murdered, and my father was charged with the crime. He was put in jail but over the next six months was found not guilty. Dad and the woman, Mary Smith, married and moved to Florida. It was only within the past several years that Mary Smith Janosik admitted that the baby she carried at the time of her husband's death was actually my half-sister.

Dad died in Florida in March, 1974. He was 73 years old. Five years later, my mother died in Petersburg, Virginia, in May of 1979. She was 72.

As complex as it could get at times, life, for the most part, was quite simple and unassuming back in the 1930s. It amazes me that life can be so hard in some respects, yet, at the same time, afford the opportunity for healing—if we are willing.

I look back and truly believe that I learned the value of unconditional love from a very unique source. She was like a sister to me and, as far as I was concerned, a part of my family. Most important, she was my friend and closest companion. Her name was Lash, and she was a beautiful English setter.

My father got Lash and trained her for hunting. She fast became a part of the community. Lash roamed freely among the nearby homes, getting fed by many of the families in the neighborhood. She was a good hunting dog. Hunting was something I learned from my father and an activity I greatly enjoyed. Eventually I took over the care of Lash, and she became my sidekick. I had a five-shot Winchester automatic shotgun and spent many hours in the woods with Lash hunting for quail.

Like everything, time took a toll on Lash. By the time she was 12 years old, she became ill, lost the full use of her legs, and could barely walk. Dad told me I had to put her down, but I simply kept putting it off. I just could not look in her eyes and find the heart to kill her even if death would have been less painful for her and more humane in the long run. Finally, Dad lost his patience with me and insisted that I do what had to be done with Lash. I went out in the woods and dug a grave while Lash innocently lay off to the side, oblivious to what was actually happening. She trusted me and

Billy Janosik, Johnny, and sister Mary sit on top of the tar paper shack that was their childhood home. A dose of healthy fear causes Johnny to inch back from the edge.

I trusted her. It broke my heart to think I was planning the execution of one of my dearest friends. The time came, and I positioned Lash's head off to the side to avoid having to see the face of my friend as I pulled the trigger. I held the gun, trembling as I aimed it at her head. I applied pressure to the trigger and, at the very moment the gun fired, Lash turned her head and looked into my eyes. The load struck her in the middle of the head and she lay silent.

I am 77 years old, and the memory of that day rings as clear in my mind as when it happened. I can still see Lash's eyes as she looked into mine at the moment I took her life. These were the trusting eyes of a friend. I want so desperately to believe that, as Dad said, I did what had to be done. All I truly know for sure is that I killed a good friend that day.

Time is the great healer. Time, however, can also be fickle. It can be both friend and foe. The most dangerous time is time wasted. I try diligently to avoid wasting time. I'm a great believer that the people who lose the most opportunities are those who "hang out" and those who sleep late.

I think growing up in poverty and being forced to work for every meal kept my family totally separated from wasted time. As I have said many times, we had to endure rough, trying times, but those times didn't mean we lacked any of the traditional fun that comes with youth.

I remember that my younger brother Billy and I wore dungarees. We hated the obnoxious outerwear which masqueraded as casual apparel. Back then, dungarees were an economic indicator crying out that the people who wore them were poor. Ironically, jeans are worn today by the masses, regardless of age or economic standing.

My younger brother Billy was a real rascal. When I think about growing up with him, I don't know whether to laugh or cry.

I was the oldest, so the chore of mowing the grass fell to me. I used a long-handled push mower with long, sharp, rotating blades. It took half a day to cut the lawn. One day, as I was cutting the grass, Billy started his usual antics; and, before long, I was pushed to my limit. We began to fight, and I chased him all over the yard with the lawn mower. As fate would have it, Billy tripped and within a split second I had almost severed two of my brother's fingers from his hand. The two digits were literally hanging by thin slits of skin. I was then in a state of panic. Fortunately for us, the insurance man was making his door-to-door collection rounds. The man grabbed Billy, wrapped his fingers tightly and then loaded him into his car and rushed Billy to the hospital. Billy's fingers were stitched and saved.

Billy never seemed to learn the art of cooperation. He was always on the lookout for trouble and was quite successful at finding it. As the older brother, the duty fell on me to try to keep this youngster in line. I was,

The Janosik family would not have been complete without beloved pet retriever, "Lash." Here Emily Janosik spends some relaxing time with three of her children, Johnny, Evelyn, Mary . . . and Lash.

therefore, the one who experienced most of the frustration. Billy really had a way of getting me riled.

Unfortunately, some of Billy's trouble making spilled over to my friends, too—like the time when my childhood friend Jack Goff got a bicycle from the Firestone store. I think the bike cost about ten dollars, and Jack's dad

Johnny's younger brother Billy with an offspring of family pet, "Lash." Johnny felt one of his key responsibilities as a young boy was to help look out for Billy.

paid fifty cents a week toward the purchase. He was the only kid in the neighborhood with a bike, so it was really exciting. We built large dirt piles and took turns riding the bicycle over the mountains of dirt.

On this one day as we rode over the dirt piles, Billy started shooting at us with a BB gun. I'm sure the pellets weren't life threatening, but they sure hurt. I stormed off the bike and headed full steam towards Billy. I struck Billy in the jaw and grabbed the gun from his hands. I wasn't aware at the moment I made contact with his jaw that Billy had his tongue between his teeth, so the impact drove his teeth through his tongue, almost cutting part of it off.

I was so frustrated with him I took the BB gun and, in an angry rage, bent it around the closest tree. The problem was that this was not Billy's gun, so I imagine he had a tough time explaining how the gun managed to be destroyed while in his possession.

I think it's normal for brothers to argue and fight while they're growing up. A point comes, however, when we reach the age where we can't imagine not getting along.

One of the times I realized how much Billy meant to me came while I was serving in the NC division aboard the USS Louisville during WWII. We'd been out to sea for over a year, and one evening, we were anchored in the Marshal Islands with a troop ship about two miles down from us. I was notified by one of the NC personnel on board my ship that someone from the troop ship was asking to speak to me. My heart literally leaped when I realized that the flickering lights from the troop ship were messages coming to me from my brother Billy. He and I spoke to one another through code lights over the Pacific Ocean. I eventually received permission to visit my brother for a short but exciting conversation aboard his troop ship. The visit was about two hours, but it seemed like only two minutes.

The bond between brothers is something special. We both endured the heartbreak of losing our mother and sisters while we were still young boys growing up in Hopewell. We stuck together and made life in that three-room tar paper shack bearable.

My brother Billy volunteered for the U.S. Navy and was excited to serve his country. If nothing else, Billy was adventuresome. He eventually came home and went to work with the Hercules Powder Company.

Life was not kind to Billy. He injured his back on the job and later developed Lou Gehrig's Disease. At the age of 47, because of the impact of this degenerative disease, Billy literally drowned in his own fluids. Recalling the last months and weeks of Billy's life as he attempted to fight off the effects of this devastating and cruel disease is heartbreaking.

I watched as Billy's body became frail and his abilities to control his movements were challenged to the point of almost immobility. As his life was slipping away, I thought about the young Billy who ran through life as if it only lasted a day—the little boy who courted trouble like a good friend.

I vividly recall the times he and I fought and wrestled in the yard, thinking then how much we hated each other. But that was as far from the truth as we could get. Our love for each other kept us together and sane during some of the toughest times either of us would ever face. It was a love born out of a true commitment to family. I only wish that this love could have saved Billy and spared him from those hard, painful last days he was forced to endure.

When I was young, I collected Star wrappers. They were found on the cover of school notebooks and could be clipped off and saved. I knew if I collected enough, I could redeem them and get a prize. I went to everybody I knew to get the Star wrappers. I had my heart set on a brand new bike at the Firestone store.

Finally, I was able to collect a thousand wrappers, enough to get the bike. What a beautiful piece of machinery I brought home that day! It had a red frame with chrome wheels, fenders, and handle bars with a basket on the front. I was really proud of that bike. It was the first and only bike I ever owned. I kept it on the porch, and it never even got so much as a rust spot.

When I left home for Laurel, Delaware, at the age of 16, I gave the bike to Billy. It was my most treasured possession. Looking back, I'm glad I gave it to someone so deserving as my little brother.

Twenty-five years ago, I had the good fortune to find a Firestone bike just like it, chrome wheels, basket and all. I think I'll pull it out of my garage, dust it off, and pump up those tires.

The hard things we have to face in life are often the very things that teach us the value of compassion and generosity. Sometimes these things are restored to us; sometimes not.

Are you facing trials and difficulties, uncertainties and tough decisions? Somewhere in the midst of it all is the chance to help others as you're making your own way in the world. There's almost no better feeling than being able to give others a boost when they need it most—except maybe the feeling of awe and satisfaction that comes over you when you discover that the person you've helped is now helping someone else.

Johnny tinkers with the bike he bought years ago at a store in Laurel. The bike is an exact replica of one he had as a youngster and eventually gave to his younger brother Billy just before heading for Delaware in 1942.

Chapter 12

A HAND UP, NOT A HAND OUT

Regardless of our economic standing, I believe we can always do something to help somebody else. The challenges brought on by a lack of financial stability in my young life will serve as a constant reminder that everyone deserves a little help when they're struggling to meet the demands of life.

Oh, I know some people abuse the system and don't take any initiative to improve themselves or make the slightest attempt to become self-sufficient. But many others could really move ahead with their lives if they just had some support and encouragement to make it past the rough spots. I'm not talking about dishing out pity or welfare but investing in people who have potential and need hope—planting seeds in the soil of their circumstances with faith that they will produce a crop of right attitudes. My experience has been that whenever I've reached out to help someone who is struggling and trying his or her best to make ends meet, I see an appreciation from them that results in a willingness to do whatever is necessary to prove the support was well invested. Plus, I can think of no greater boost to my own feeling of self worth than that which comes from helping someone to succeed.

You might think this sounds corny, but I'm convinced that helping others is a way to help myself. I would feel like a thief if I didn't use the fruits of my life's labors to develop resources for people in need. I have been truly blessed. I willingly admit that I'm far from the most intelligent man in the world, but God blessed me with a desire to work twice as hard to make up for what I may lack. So in the spirit of our commitment to continue paying "life's tuition," my wife and I have dedicated our available financial and physical resources to several special charity opportunities.

I have a special place in my heart for my community. Over the past 60 years, Laurel, Delaware, has become my home; and I have a deep appreciation for the people. Laurel is where a third generation Slovak immigrant has been able to chase the "American dream" and through hard work and dedication, catch it. I owe it to my community to do whatever I can to help it grow and prosper. This is the reason that about twelve years ago I joined a grass roots community revitalization effort that has been instrumental in bringing about positive economic and aesthetic change in the town of Laurel. The Laurel Redevelopment Corporation (LRC) was started by about a dozen area businesspeople that were concerned with maintaining the economic viability of the community.

Over the years, certain parts of the town have fallen victim to abandoned commercial and residential properties that were left in a serious state of disrepair. In the 1980s, the once prosperous downtown area, where I had previously owned several buildings, was overshadowed by large slum-like brick buildings that were largely occupied by drug dealers and users.

As members of LRC, we combined our financial resources to create a non-profit agency that would work to purchase the dilapidated buildings and either restore or demolish them. Our first major project was to purchase the row of brick buildings that were once home to several major Laurel businesses, including Johnny Janosik TV and Appliances.

The LRC bought the buildings and demolished them. Today, in a place where it was once unsafe to walk for fear of either being subjected to some rather seedy characters or having a brick from the top level of the building fall on you, you see a wonderful, spacious community park. The Market Square Park serves as a comfortable place to relax or listen to entertainment from the large bandstand that is situated in the park.

When I was asked to join the LRC, about 15 local businesspeople were involved; each one had pledged to contribute $10,000 to the project. In order to make sure the organization remained financially solvent and to get the money so the necessary work could start, I set out to help collect funds. Aware that people don't like to be bothered during breakfast or dinner, I went out two days a week from about 10 a.m. to 2 p.m.

I served as the mouthpiece of the LRC, carrying the message to the people about the importance of helping assure that Laurel maintained its tradition of a clean, enhanced quality of life. While I was told that some of the people who were most able to afford to be involved in this project might be the hardest ones to convince, I found that people just needed to be approached in a way that appealed to their point of view. Everybody wanted Laurel to survive and prosper; we just needed to sell the LRC concept in a way they could appreciate.

The idea must have worked because, within two weeks, the people of Laurel pledged $300,000 to the LRC mission. Some were the $10,000 contributors, but others were able to invest $1,000 and still get a vote at LRC meetings.

I'm excited about what the LRC has been able to accomplish in the community. Along with the Market Street Park, the LRC has converted overgrown, open fields and dilapidated homes and businesses into a major business complex called LaurelTown. About nine businesses occupy LaurelTown with goods ranging from jewelry to baby items. Across the street from LaurelTown's main business complex is a large restaurant. R. J. Riverside, which sits on the banks of Broad Creek. Broad Creek is a tributary of the Nanticoke River, which runs into the Chesapeake Bay.

We also became concerned about deteriorating conditions along an area on Front Street and the impending threat of a pollution problem with Broad Creek. The LRC bought the property, cleaned it up, and it now houses another community park. Broad Creek runs clear.

I'm particularly proud of this because of my involvement in developing the park. I took three employees from my business and, using LRC funds, we physically and mentally built that park. I'm gifted with the ability to create a vision in my mind of how I want to see a property develop; and, with the exception of meeting code, I don't even have to draw out plans. I just work from my mind. We installed a brick walkway and placed park benches and other amenities on the park property. Some people in town jokingly call it "Janosik Park" because of my involvement in the project.

Over the years, it has been my family's policy to keep our community service and philanthropic efforts anonymous. I believe that God appreciates the work we do for others even more when we do it without seeking personal attention or some sense of fame.

Recently, however, I have to admit that I was completely overwhelmed by a show of appreciation that came from the community of Laurel. I've always enjoyed my association with the Laurel Redevelopment Corporation and feel the community revitalization work we've been able to accomplish has been remarkable and much needed. This organization has been a true example of team effort among the leadership and members, and my family and I have always enjoyed being a part of it.

Since I pride myself on staying involved in the community and in touch with the people, many of them longtime friends, little occurs in the small town of Laurel that I'm not privy to. That certainly changed one evening in December 2002.

My family told me that I was to attend a special staff Christmas party hosted by Bev Hastings, my friend and Johnny Janosik store employee, at R. J. Riverside restaurant. When we arrived at the restaurant, I was surprised to see so many vehicles in the parking lot.

As we walked through the doors of the restaurant's banquet room, I was shocked to find over 200 people staring at me. It took a few seconds to gain my composure as it dawned on me that everyone was there in my honor. I couldn't fathom that this many people (some I hadn't seen in years and others who, quite frankly, I thought didn't care for me) were there on my behalf. I was humbled.

My colleagues in the LRC explained that the evening was planned as a tribute to show appreciation for the community service that my family and I have given to Laurel over the years. This tribute came in the form of a park dedication. It's a wonderful feeling to know that people appreciate you, and words can't express how nice it is for friends to show it like they did that evening.

The level of emotion went even higher as I realized that my family name would be recognized forever on a bronze plaque to be placed at the entrance of a park in the town of Laurel. The park chosen is also very special because it's the very LRC project that I personally developed, designed, and built with the help of some employees from the Johnny Janosik business.

It's obvious that the name Janosik does not ring out as a traditional Laurel or Sussex County family name. However, because the people of this community were willing to show true compassion and friendship over the years since I arrived in 1942, my family name is now a true part of the history of this wonderful community.

The LRC has also restored several businesses along Laurel's traditional downtown on Market Street. The organization owns and maintains its properties as commercial rentals. This ownership helps to provide the necessary capital to continue our revitalization efforts. In all, the LRC has completed work that has added about $6 million in economic stimulus for the Laurel area. It's exciting to be a part of the valuable work being performed by the LRC to help beautify and revitalize the community of Laurel.

The same is true about probably my favorite charity project, the Good Samaritan Aid Organization. Members of a local church started the Good Samaritan many years ago, and the organization provides a huge amount of support for families in need. About the time we were getting the LRC started, someone approached me about serving on the board of the Good Samaritan.

The LRC had recently purchased the vacant commercial buildings downtown, and the Good Samaritan was operating out of a building right across the street from where we were developing Market Square Park. The Good Samaritan operates a second hand thrift shop using items donated by members of the community. The funds raised from the store provide the resources that help local families meet medical, food, clothing, and household needs.

The Good Samaritan shop was bursting at the seams, having grown far too large for the 800 square-foot building it occupied. Just down the street, a furniture store had gone out of business, and the 5,000 square-foot building was being sold for about $90,000. I spoke to the owners of the building and they told me they would carry the mortgage for five years at eight percent interest. I knew that if the Good Samaritan got into a larger building, it could increase sales and profits by a substantial margin.

I convinced the board of the Good Samaritan to sell its small building to the LRC for $20,000. With the additional $5,000 that Mary Louise and I donated, the Good Samaritan was able to put $10,000 down on the furniture building and still have money left over to cover operations and moving costs. The Good Samaritan moved and, as predicted, sales increased. Within four and a half years the store paid off its $80,000 mortgage.

I enjoy my involvement with the Good Samaritan because it's doing the type of goodwill work that is needed badly by many people. I've been working as Outreach Coordinator for the past couple of years, and this job allows me to talk to and work with the people whose needs the Good Samaritan is meeting.

Each day I visit the store before it opens and listen to the messages left on the telephone answering machine from people who need help with everything from electric bills to prescription medicine. The Good Samaritan has been so successful in its charity mission that many social organizations throughout the State of Delaware contact us when seeking help for their clients. I'm usually able to sift through the calls and find ways to help the families who are facing serious challenges. In cases where families have been burned out of their homes, my daughter Lori works from the Johnny Janosik store to coordinate donations of furniture to help them get back on their feet. When I'm not completely sure how to address certain needs, I work closely with the Delaware Social

Johnny and Mary Louise Janosik and their family were honored at a special park dedication ceremony held in Laurel in December 2002. At the ceremony, the Laurel Redevelopment Corporation dedicated one of the parks that was developed under Johnny's supervision. Pictured are (left to right): John Hollis, Delaware Community Foundation; State Senator Bob Venables; Linda Janosik Christophel; Mary Louise and Johnny Janosik; Don Phillips, President of the LRC; John Shwed, President of the Laurel Community Foundation; Kathy Wooten of the Delaware State Service Center in Laurel; Donald Dykes, President of the Board of the Laurel Good Samaritan; Lori Janosik Morrison and husband Barry; and Ed Hannigan, President of the Laurel Chamber of Commerce.

Services Center, and they help by connecting people with the most suitable support agency.

Working as outreach coordinator for the Good Samaritan makes me feel good about what we're doing for many families in the area, but it also exposes me to just how hard a life some people have. It's sad to know that in a time when many opportunities are available, still some fall through the cracks and deep into tough times. But we have to feel fortunate that we're able to touch as many people as we do.

It's really a great experience to be a part of the annual Christmas Basket project that has been a part of Laurel's holiday setting for the past 15 years or so. Volunteers get together and fill between 250 and 300 baskets with food items including canned goods, chicken, ham, bread, butter and milk. Local ministers refer needy families to the State Service Center, and the baskets are delivered to them just before Christmas.

What really makes Samaritan successful is the number of people who care enough to volunteer their time. A few years ago, the Salvation Army stopped its 15-year tradition of the holiday "bell ringer" drive at a local grocery store. Seeing this as an opportunity for raising operational funds for the Good Samaritan, I helped to organize our local people as volunteers to become bell ringers at the store. We now have 100 people who volunteer time from Thanksgiving through Christmas to ring the bell to raise money for Good Samaritan. Our most recent effort raised $11,000. Our local people support this charity fund-raiser in a big way. Ironically enough, the people with the least amount of money give the most.

With the thrift store operation and the holiday bell ringing effort, the Good Samaritan is doing very well in terms of maintaining a strong financial base. This enabled us to use the Good Samaritan to help support another charity project in the community, the Hope

House project. Hope House consists of four transitional homes for people who are faced with emergency situations that resulted in the loss of housing. The State Service Center determines who is eligible for access to Hope House, and we formed the Laurel Foundation to handle maintenance and operation of the shelters.

The great thing about Hope House, along with its obvious benefit to people in need, is the partnership that local organizations have established to keep it running. It costs $24,000 a year to maintain operations at the four Hope House units; Good Samaritan contributes $6,000, and local churches and civic organizations support the project. We also designate $6,000 of the holiday bell ringing funds toward the project.

I know that the Hope House project is doing wonderful things in the community. As a matter of fact, I was so impressed with the project that, when I learned about problems raising funds to build the last two housing units, I became personally committed to making sure they would be completed. I took responsibility for contracting out the construction work and donated finances. Believe me, this money and time was well spent.

I think the most rewarding part of working with these Laurel charity efforts is watching the entire community come together to be sure resources are available for people in need. This is one of the best examples of why I've come to love this little town and am proud to call it home for so many years. My appreciation for the people and community of Laurel drives me to stay involved in projects that help it grow.

I have a special place in my heart for the children who are growing up in our area. I know without a doubt that, as we have heard so many times, children are our future. My family and I want to make sure that young people get every opportunity to be successful and live happy, productive lives.

Even as a young boy, I knew that education would be my key to life. We cannot minimize the importance of education in a young person's life. Many kids have great potential, and I want to help them when they need that extra push. Some kids will fall through the cracks because of economic and social disadvantages, while others may possess challenges in their own abilities to learn. Whatever the case, we have to work to find ways to avoid the stumbling block of any child missing out on the opportunity to be successful in the classroom and eventually in life itself.

That's why my wife and I started the Janosik Family Charitable Foundation. The Foundation provides a vehicle to help support educational initiatives in the community. The Janosik Family Charitable Foundation is committed to supporting educational efforts including our local library, school programs, and special education initiatives. I've always felt strongly about the need for education, but I've become even more active in this since learning that one of my grandchildren was diagnosed with Attention Deficit Disorder. My granddaughter is a beautiful little girl, with all the excitement and playfulness that comes with being an eight-year-old. But she has a learning disability that could easily keep her from achieving her full potential. Her mother has worked exceptionally hard to develop special education initiatives at a local private Christian school, and the results have been great. Special education opportunities go a long way toward helping children be successful in the classroom.

It's my goal to keep education as a primary focus so we can keep as few kids as possible from falling through the cracks. So many grown-ups look back on their childhood school experiences and wish they had paid better attention in class. Let's do everything we can to help today's youth appreciate and enjoy the many educational opportunities open to them.

Someone recently asked me, "If you had it to do over again, is there anything you would do differently in your life?" Hmm. Good question. What about you? Oh, there might be some things we'd want to do over. But for the most part, I'd venture to say that most of us did the best we could at any given moment with what we knew and what we had to deal with.

Have you given much thought to the influence the people and places of your childhood have had on you? Have you ever considered going back to where you grew up and looking around at how things have changed over the years? I did. It's funny how different things seem when you're older and taller.

Dear Mary and Johnny Janosik,

I used to work for your business as a "Greeter" in 1996 and 1997. At Christmas time you were so kind as to help me get into my trailer and help my children have a Christmas. I am just writing to let you know that I have never forgotten your help and your kindness.

I was talking to my friend who works at your stores. I let her know that I have been wanting to thank you and let you know that I have never forgotten the wonderful things you helped me and my children with. She encouraged me to go ahead and do what my heart tells me to do and write to you. So, I am saying thank you so much and may God bless you both.

A letter received by Johnny and Mary Janosik from a former employee

Chapter 13

YOU CAN NEVER GO HOME

I've heard it said many times that you can never go home. More than ever I find that statement to be true. Since becoming involved in writing this book and recounting the events of my life, a number of different emotions have stirred within me. And it created a strong desire to revisit my past. So I ventured back down to my hometown of Hopewell, Virginia.

My sisters Mary and Evelyn never left the Hopewell area, and both remain in Prince George's County. Mary, my older sister, still lives within 10 miles of our old birth home, and my younger sister Evelyn lives about 25 miles away in Dinwittie. I have visited my sisters and their families on many occasions; however, I never really took the proverbial "trip down memory lane" and visited some of the landmarks of my youth.

Traveling down U.S. 13 toward Virginia, I realized that today's trip would be different from any other I had ever taken. This time, I would not only be visiting my sisters but my past. This time, I realized, I would look at the city of Hopewell through different eyes. I would try to see it as I did over 60 yeas ago.

Grayson Hurley, friend and Johnny Janosik employee, accompanied me on this trip. Grayson does a variety of jobs around the grounds of the business, as well as some personal landscaping and maintenance duties for my family and me. I figured it would be wise to have Grayson drive while I tried to find some of the places that by now would be hidden by over 60 years of growth and development. This turned out to be a wise decision.

JOSEPH R. BIDEN, JR.
DELAWARE

1105 NORTH MARKET STREET
SUITE 2000
WILMINGTON, DELAWARE 19801-1233
(302) 573-6345

United States Senate

JUDICIARY COMMITTEE
SUBCOMMITTEE ON
CRIME AND DRUGS
CHAIRMAN

FOREIGN RELATIONS COMMITTEE
CHAIRMAN

CAUCUS ON INTERNATIONAL
NARCOTICS CONTROL
CHAIRMAN

December 2, 2002

Mr. Johnny Janosik
c/o Mr. Tony Windsor
110 Pennsylvania Ave.
Seaford, DE 19973

Dear Mr. Janosik:

    I am writing to congratulate you on the dedication of a park in your honor. It is a pleasure to know that someone who has given so much to the people of Delaware is being acknowledged for his service.

    From your charitable business practices to your involvement with community organizations like the Good Samaritan Shop and Hope House, your deeds speak volumes about your commitment to the community. It is both comforting and inspiring to know that folks like you are out there, making the world a better place for those in need.

    As your friends and neighbors honor you this evening, you will see that efforts such as yours do not go unnoticed. Keep up the good work, and don't hesitate to let me know how you're doing.

Sincerely,

Joseph R. Biden, Jr.
United States Senator

Besides, both my sisters live in homes with large yards and both needed new lawn mowers. Since I had two John Deere models on hand, I thought it would be good to take them down and deliver them during our visit. So Grayson and I set out on our trip in my daughter's SUV, pulling a trailer with the two lawn mowers. I had not seen my sisters in a while, and I was really looking forward to the reunion.

When we arrived at Mary's home, we shared a lunch and looked over some of the old family pictures she had on hand. As we went outside to take a look at the lawn mower I had brought for her, we walked past a huge field behind her house. It was the same field where I worked as a young boy hoeing peanuts. Before I could hoe the peanuts, I had to walk the entire length of that field with a mule, a distance which seemed to me at the time like five to ten miles. The length was actually about one mile.

After getting the lawn mower situated, I headed for Evelyn's home. I was happy to find that my niece Janey and her husband Cecil were also home with their daughter Sheryl.

Cecil is an avid Civil War buff and has visited many of the Virginia battlefields in search of historic remnants of the war. He has a collection that includes literally

Johnny with sister Evelyn Janosik Brown. Evelyn still resides near the family's hometown of Hopewell, Virginia.

hundreds of Civil War pieces he has dug up out of the ground and taken off creek bottoms.

His collection includes weapons, uniforms, buttons, badges and ammunition from both small and large firearms. During one visit to a local historic site, Cecil actually discovered the skeletal remains of a Confederate soldier, including his uniform and all the accompanying war pins and badges. His vast knowledge of the Civil War and extensive collection of artifacts is amazing.

Johnny and sister Mary Janosik Basil. Mary still resides near her family's home in Hopewell, Virginia.

My sister, along with her husband, Junior, and Janey decided to make the trip to Hopewell with me to help me get my bearings and find some of the old spots—another wise decision. As we headed out along Route 460, I developed a sense of excitement, anticipation, and a strange sort of dread—almost the same anxious feelings I had as the Greyhound bus brought me into the town of Laurel and a new life back in 1942.

As we drove down Route 36 and into the city of Hopewell, I was totally lost. Nothing seemed familiar. I remember peanut fields, small stores, and dirt roads. Now, I saw Shoney's, Blockbuster, Taco Bell, and every type of motel chain imaginable. I quickly realized that while I was growing and developing my life and business back in Laurel, my hometown was also going through a massive growth spurt.

Coming into Hopewell, we passed over a small bridge and what I remember as Yellow Belly Creek, a favorite swimming hole for the local kids. The area was completely overgrown with brush and trees, and I could barely make out the small stream of water and surrounding area that was now a state bird sanctuary. I remember Yellow Belly Creek as the place where the guys would go "buck bathing," hoping to get out before the girls got to the creek. Evelyn recalled how the kids would slide down the clay hills surrounding the creek and their bathing suits would get filthy from the muddy red clay.

We stopped at the intersection of South 15th Avenue and Arlington Road. I suddenly recalled an incident that I am not particularly proud of today. I can still see the man approaching my friends and me and asking if we would help load crates of fireworks into his truck. Typically, businesspeople solicited the help of young kids and then conveniently forgot to pay them. So, being sure not to fall to this fate, we began loading the fireworks; however, for every five or six boxes we loaded into the truck, we'd put one box into our wagon. After the job was complete, we realized what would happen if our criminal activities were discovered by our parents. So we headed down to Yellow Belly Creek and spent the evening setting off fireworks to destroy the evidence.

I could not believe how well preserved old man Frank Dereski's store had remained. Today it's a nursery, hardwood, and mulch facility. When I was growing up in Hopewell, this was a general store where we would shop for food; but it was also one of our childhood destinations for candy. Looking into the plate glass windows of the building, I'm convinced that the same counter and shelves still remain in the empty Dereski building. One feature that made Dereski's Store a necessary destination for my family was the fact that in the 1930s Mr. Dereski allowed our family and most others in this poor industrial town to have a line of credit. I could ride my bike down to Dereski's with a list from my mother and get the food without having to pay until the end of the month—or whenever Mom and Dad got the money. This credit was a big help to my mother while Dad was working away in Brazil.

Johnny stands on the banks of what used to be called "Yellow Belly Creek." As youngsters, he and his friends would swim in the waters of this stream. Today the creek is part of a bird sanctuary.

Mr. Dereski also had a sawmill behind the store, and I worked there sometimes as a boy. On Saturdays, a couple of friends and I would cut up wood slabs for firewood. The work was very hard, and my fingers would almost bleed before the day was done. Looking back now, I can see just how beneficial this job was for Mr. Dereski. We would work 4-6 hours and Mr. Dereski would pay us about 30 cents. We would then clamor into his store and spend the money on BB Bats (a hard caramel candy on a stick). It would take over an hour to finish off the candy, but it was a treat that my friends and I were able to share. We'd take turns licking the BB Bats, getting angry if one of us took more than one lick.

Driving through Hopewell, it was a blow to find that the woods and fields were now populated with interstates, bypasses, and an assortment of major businesses. The area is now a metropolis, and people are everywhere. I tried my best to find landmarks; but, with all the development, it was pretty nearly impossible to find anything that I could recognize.

As we rounded a corner, I suddenly caught site of a very familiar site, the old Hopewell High School. Except for being somewhat run down and having broken doors and windows, it looked the same as the day I graduated from the 11th grade. The huge brick building with the horseshoe drive was just like a picture from my past. What a find!

I walked around to the back of the school, where another major reminder still stood like a friend from my youth. It was the same eight-foot high concrete fence that was built around the school's football field back in 1938. I think it cost a nickel to get into the games, but most of us were so poor we couldn't even afford that. Guys would stand on each other's shoulders to watch the game and try to sneak in. I remember when the fence was being built. The project fell under the federal government's Works Project Administration (WPA), an initiative that created work for people who were unemployed after the

During a visit to his hometown of Hopewell, Virginia, Johnny stopped at the site of the former "Dereski's Store," where his family bought much of its food.

Recently, Johnny visited his former high school, Hopewell High School in Virginia. He graduated in 1941 with the required eleven years of education.

During the 1930s, Johnny's father, John, was able to get work helping to build an eight-foot concrete wall that surrounded the Hopewell High School football field. In 2002, Johnny took time to visit the high school and the wall.

depression. My father worked some of the WPA projects.

Two other buildings that have changed little over the years are St. James Parochial School, where I attended elementary school, and the Catholic convent next door. The red brick walls are every bit as solid as they were when I was filing down the hallways and playing on the playground. The school's original upstairs was a church that almost crumbled at one time; the entire second floor was taken off the building. Today the school bears the title of St. James Youth Center. It appears, however, that the center has closed and the future of the building is uncertain. The building stands in an extremely busy part of the city of Hopewell. The convent next door seems so much smaller than it did when I was a youngster.

Today, standing on the steps where my class gathered for a photograph to commemorate our graduation on to high school, I find it hard to imagine that these two modest buildings hold such a large place in my heart and memories.

Leaving the site of St. James, I couldn't help but pass by the old Street Car Station. The building has been remodeled and looks very nice sitting off to the side of the busy highway.

I can remember well walking to the station to catch the streetcar to grade school. Even though the walk to the streetcar station was probably a farther distance than the walk from home to school, that walk kept us from

Johnny visited Hopewell, Virginia, in the summer of 2002. Here he stops to spend time at St. Mary's convent where he attended school.

A beaming Johnny Janosik (second row, extreme right) holds his diploma while his graduating class of St. James Catholic School have their photo taken.

Pictured here is Johnny's childhood primary school, St. James Catholic School in Hopewell, Virginia. Currently the facility serves as a youth center.

Chapter 13 • You Can Never Go Home 131

having to cross through the many wooded areas and fields and also allowed us to share some social times with our friends before getting to school.

Without a doubt, the highlight of my visit to Hopewell came when we pulled up in front of the property where I lived as a child. It was High Street when I was growing up there, but today it's called Stewart Street. The part of the yard that once housed the tar paper shack is vacant, but the home that we built still stands nearby with a few minor renovations.

What a strange feeling to walk across the yard where I had played over 60 years ago! I walked around the empty house and found that a section of roof had been removed and the back porch where I parked my bike for the last time before leaving home for Laurel was no longer attached to the home.

In the summer of 2002, Johnny visited his childhood home in Hopewell, Virginia.

The door and steps to the basement were still there, as well as a few other remnants. Returning to Hopewell allowed me to reflect on just how much positive development has taken place. The community is beautiful. It's obvious to me that, over the years, the city has been able to clean up some of the negative environmental effects that were starting to be a concern before I left. I applaud the people of the

Hopewell area for the wonderful things they've done in the community, and I certainly look forward to making more trips back in the near future.

With all that change, it was difficult for me to picture everything as it was—I've been gone for many years, and memory has a habit of switching things around on us. As I stood and looked out over that yard that was once my childhood home, however, in my mind I clearly saw my mother and father and my brother and sisters just as they appeared many years ago. I know the "home" of our childhood will never be the same, but for a brief few moments I was as close as I could ever hope to be.

If you want
an hour of happiness,
take a nap.

If you want
a week of happiness,
take a vacation.

If you want
a lifetime of happiness,
help someone else.

Chapter 14

CONCLUDING THOUGHTS

Where has the time gone? Now in my late 70s, I'm able to recall things that seem almost impossible for my grandchildren to imagine. They wonder how I was able to survive without computers, cell phones, video games, electricity, or indoor plumbing.

I take solace in knowing that even though times and societies have changed and technology has advanced us to a new level, the fundamental principals of life remain the same. As hard a concept as it may be for some people to grasp, compassion and charitable generosity are the true marks of success.

The Lord has blessed me and my family with a successful business and good, hard-working employees. As important as the business is, my blessings far surpass the walls of the Johnny Janosik store. I have been blessed with a loving family, good friends, and opportunities. Believe me, over the years I've held tightly to all of these blessings and taken full advantage of the benefits they bring.

More often than not, people tend to think of money as the basis for their definition of success. I would certainly be a hypocrite if

I didn't admit that financial success has allowed my family and me to have advantages that others may not be able to enjoy. Worse than being a hypocrite, however, it would be almost criminal if I didn't use my financial success to help others. To me, the most rewarding part of success is that it puts me in a position to help others.

You don't have to be rich to be compassionate and caring. Regardless of our economic standing, we all have the capacity to reach out and encourage someone in need. We have the ability to become involved in a child's life and help him or her learn the difference between right and wrong. These are the simple, fundamental, important principles of life.

Many times, we take ourselves far too seriously and lack the ability to be humble. I'm convinced that this world has basically two types of people—the givers and the takers. The people who fail to find humor in themselves and who demonstrate an attitude of callousness are more often than not "takers."

I like to suggest that people try a little test that I often take to assure I don't take myself too seriously. Go into the bathroom, close the door, and look into the mirror. As you stare into your own reflection, repeat, "You dummy, you dummy, you dummy." If, after a few seconds or certainly a couple of minutes, you don't find yourself laughing, it's possible you're a taker. Now, to double check your humility level if you didn't find yourself laughing, take off all your clothes and once again stare into the mirror and say, "You dummy, you dummy, you dummy." I assure you, this test has not only resulted in my laughing hysterically but has also led to my taking many showers in the dark.

This example is certainly intended as an exercise in humor; but actually, the point I'm trying to make is that we each have a responsibility to keep ourselves humble. If we can be the kind of people who care more about helping others than ourselves, then the difference we can make in an often-cruel society will be phenomenal.

I enjoy an old adage I once read. The author is unknown, but the concept is wonderful. It goes like this:

If you want an hour of happiness, take a nap.
If you want a week of happiness, take a vacation.
If you want a lifetime of happiness, help someone else.

I've been invited to speak to students at various schools in my area and find this to be a remarkable experience. Nothing is more exciting than to look into the eyes of young people whose lives really have yet to begin. I want, with every ounce of conviction in me, for these youth to recognize the wonderful opportunities that lie before them.

If only the young people I talk to could know just how fortunate they are to be growing up in the United States. First of all, they're blessed to be living in a country that allows them the freedom to pursue their dreams. I will be forever grateful to my grandfather for accepting the struggle and hardships that must have accompanied his decision to bring his family to America. Even when I was a young boy, I recognized the enormous responsibility that comes with the freedom that U.S. citizens enjoy. Nothing in life is free, and the road to success is filled with many obstacles and challenges; however, having the freedom that America provides gives us a real jump-start.

I cannot stress enough the importance of hard work and determination in the formula for success. In addition, here are a few other things to keep in mind as you pursue your goals and dreams:

1. *Develop a vision.*
   Recognize what it is that you want to accomplish, develop a plan, and work the plan. Don't spend a lot of time looking for shortcuts. In the long run, you will save time by doing it right the first time.

2. *Learn a lesson.*
   Every experience, whether good or bad, contains a lesson. Make sure that no experience is wasted; instead, recognize each one as a learning opportunity.

3. *Ask for help.*
   If you don't understand something, ask someone who knows. Never be embarrassed to admit that you do not know everything. Don't waste valuable time becoming frustrated; simply ask for help.

4. *Take time to be kind.*
   Recognize the importance of sharing your talents. Reaching out with encouraging words or deeds, will really help you sleep at night. And if you should be blessed with financial success, remember, money is only as good as the good you can do with it. Supporting charity is the greatest "feel good" medicine in the world.

5. *Stay busy.*
   Don't dry up on the vine. Keep looking for opportunities to be productive. Real success is not a part-time job!

6. *Show appreciation.*
   Let people know how much you appreciate their help and support. Say "thank you" as if you mean it! Never let time separate you and your family and friends; remember, people are life's real blessings.

7. *Pray.*
   Pray as though your life depends on it. It does.

8. *Go back to the basics.*
   Always remember when times get tough, whether in your business life or your personal life, to step back, take a deep breath, and go back to the basics:

   - Be honest.
   - Be fair.
   - Be willing to give great service.

Everybody wants to be appreciated and respected, so I promise that this philosophy will work every time.

God bless, and thanks for listening!

LEFT: Johnny talks with Donald Dykes, President of the Laurel Good Samaritan Aid Organization Board of Directors. For years, Johnny and his family have supported the organization which provides over $100,000 in financial and material resources for needy families in southern Delaware.

RIGHT: Laurel Community Foundation president John Schwed and board member Kathy Wooten are grateful to Johnny and his family for being longtime supporters. The Foundation provides emergency, transitional shelter for individuals and families in need.

LEFT: The Janosik Family Charitable Foundation has earmarked funding opportunities for education, including construction of Delmarva Christian High School in Georgetown, Delaware. The school will provide faith-based education to students in grades 9-12. Here, Johnny is briefed on the progress of the school construction by DCHS board member Steve Theis (far right) and school principal W. Scott Kemerling.

RIGHT: The Janosiks are affiliated with Our Lady of Lourdes Catholic Church in Seaford, Delaware. Here Johnny talks with Father John Harrison, parish priest, about a major project to build an elementary school on the Delmarva Peninsula.

LEFT: This is one of two sanitary trucks owned by the Johnny Janosik furniture business. Johnny delights in donating the two trucks and drivers to help the Laurel community with annual town-wide clean up projects.

RIGHT: Bob Durham, Vice-Chairman of the Laurel Redevelopment Corporation, stops to talk with Johnny outside the LaurelTown business complex in downtown Laurel. Johnny is an active member of the LRC, an organization that has developed several major commercial and residential properties in the community, including LaurelTown.

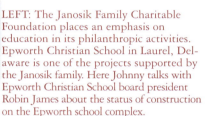

LEFT: The Janosik Family Charitable Foundation places an emphasis on education in its philanthropic activities. Epworth Christian School in Laurel, Delaware is one of the projects supported by the Janosik family. Here Johnny talks with Epworth Christian School board president Robin James about the status of construction on the Epworth school complex.

RIGHT: The Janosik Family Charitable Foundation contributed funds for Peninsula Regional Medical Center in Salisbury, Md., to purchase a state-of-the-art robotic arm to assist cardiac physicians in performing minimally invasive surgeries. Johnny has had several surgeries at PRMC, including heart bypass and shoulder replacement. Here the Janosiks present a check to PRMC on behalf of the Janosik Family Charitable Foundation. From left are: Dr. Barry Morrison, Lori Janosik-Morrison, Dr. Michael Buchness, Mary Janosik, Johnny Janosik and Jeannie Ruff, director of cardiovascular and pulmonary rehab.

LEFT: Ed Ralph, president of the Board of Commissioners of the Laurel Library and Tamatha Lambert, library director, study plans with Johnny for a new $1 million expansion to the library. Supported by the Janosik family's Charitable Foundation, contstruction plans include a room in honor of Mary Louise Janosik's parents, Norman and Lulu Hedges.